Sirach

Guides to Apocrypha and Pseudepigrapha
Series Editor
Michael A. Knibb

SIRACH

Richard J. Coggins

Copyright © 1998 Sheffield Academic Press

Published by Sheffield Academic Press Ltd
Mansion House
19 Kingfield Road
Sheffield S11 9AS
England

Printed on acid-free paper in Great Britain
by The Cromwell Press
Trowbridge, Wiltshire

British Library Cataloguing in Publication Data

A catalogue record for this book is available
from the British Library

ISBN 1-85075-7658

Contents

Preface	7
Commentaries and Other Important Studies	9
Abbreviations	11
1. Introduction	13
Title	14
Chapter and Verse Enumeration	17
Date	18
Canonicity	20
2. Structure and Contents	23
Literary Forms	23
Structure	24
Contents	26
3. The Languages of the Book	33
The Hebrew Text	34
The Greek Text and Other Translations	37
Textual Criticism	38
4. The Social and Religious Background of Sirach	42
Second Temple Judaism	43
The Geographical Setting	45
Sirach's Professional Status	48
Sirach and Hellenism	50
5. Sirach within Judaism	56
Sirach and the Parties within Judaism	57
6. Use of 'Scripture'	62
Biblical Quotations in Sirach?	62
Sirach and Proverbs	65
Other Biblical Links	66
7. Setting: The Development of the Wisdom Tradition	70
A School Setting?	70
Sirach and the Apocalyptic Tradition	73
The Figure of Wisdom	75

8. Praise of the Ancestors	78
9. Attitude to Women	85
Human Women Negatively Judged	85
Woman Wisdom	90
10. Theological Themes	92
The Fear of the Lord	94
History and Creation	95
Wisdom	96
Other Theological Concerns	99
Appendix A: The English Versions	102
Appendix B: Survey of Research	105
Other Reference Tools	106
Index of References	107
Index of Authors	110

Preface

One obvious qualification for writing a Guide of this type is that one has already engaged in extensive research, a doctoral thesis or the like, on the text to which the Guide is offered. But it may also be useful to invite someone whose scholarly concerns have previously been in more or less closely related areas to come to study a text, to see what problems he or she discovers, to assess the existing literature on that text.

This Guide comes very much in that second category. During my time at King's College London I once or twice had the somewhat alarming privilege of leading Professor Michael Knibb's 'Intertestamental Studies' seminar in exploring Sirach, but I could not claim to have engaged in serious independent research on the book. So it was an exciting but also distinctly challenging task with which I found myself confronted when Professor Knibb invited me to contribute this Study Guide.

Some of the texts covered in this series are the concerns of distinctively specialist interests, with relatively small bibliographies. Sirach, by contrast, has attracted attention from many different quarters. Those who are concerned with the Wisdom literature of the Hebrew Bible have usually gone on to discuss Sirach. Those who are studying the development of Judaism at the turn of the eras have often made Sirach their starting-point. The phenomenon of a text originally written in Hebrew but handed down in Greek has attracted discussion. And so on: Sirach has been the subject of a great deal of scholarly interest in recent years.

These points are mentioned at this stage mainly in order to explain the nature of the bibliographical references in this Guide. At first it was hoped to provide a consolidated bibliography at the end of the book, but it soon became clear that the size of such a bibliography would soon outrun its usefulness. What is provided, therefore, is a short list of commentaries and other important studies, immediately following this Preface, together with 'Further Reading' at the end of each chapter. These lists of 'Further Reading' refer specifically to works that have been mentioned in that chapter.

It remains only for me to express my thanks to Michael Knibb for the initial invitation, for his patience when the manuscript took longer to arrive than he had envisaged, and for his very helpful comments on its first draft. Among various colleagues and friends who have provided assistance and encouragement I should particularly wish to single out Dr Graham Gould of King's; Dr Sarah Pearce of the University of Southampton; and Dr Charlotte Hempel, now of Lucy Cavendish College, Cambridge, for their help in making available information that was not easily accessible to one working a long way from a biblical studies library.

Commentaries and Other Important Studies

There are not many recent commentaries on Sirach. In English it seems that only two independent works have appeared in the last 25 years. Much the more substantial of these is that started by P.W. Skehan, and taken over following his death by A.A. Di Lella, *The Wisdom of Ben Sira* (AB, 39; New York: Doubleday, 1987). This will certainly be a major resource for any detailed study of Sirach.

On a smaller scale, but very useful as a first introduction to the book, is J.G. Snaith, *Ecclesiasticus* (Cambridge Bible Commentary on the New English Bible; Cambridge: Cambridge University Press, 1974).

Other Commentaries

G.H. Box and W.O.E. Oesterley, 'Sirach', in *APOT*, I, pp. 268-517.

R. Smend, *Die Weisheit des Jesus Sirach* (3 vols.; Berlin: W. de Gruyter, 1906–1907).

C. Spicq, *L'Ecclésiastique* (La Sainte Bible; Paris: Letouzey et Ané, 1951).

A.A. Di Lella, 'Sirach', in *The New Jerome Bible Commentary* (London: Geoffrey Chapman, 1989), pp. 496-509. Very brief, but a useful introduction to his more extensive work in the AB volume.

Two other types of work are useful for those coming to the study of Sirach. The first is related to ancient Israel's Wisdom literature. Here special mention should be made of G. von Rad, *Wisdom in Israel* (London: SCM Press, 1972), which may be said to have set the agenda for much subsequent study. Pages 240-62 deal specifically with Sirach, but it would be desirable to read the whole book if possible. There are many smaller introductions to Wisdom literature; one that I have found very helpful is R.E. Murphy, *The Tree of Life* (Grand Rapids: Eerdmans, 2nd edn, 1996). The original edition was published in 1990, but the second edition contains a useful supplement.

The other type of writing that one should bear in mind is that concerned with the history, and particularly the religious history, of the

Hellenistic period. A good handbook on the historical side is L.L. Grabbe, *Judaism from Cyrus to Hadrian* (Minneapolis: Fortress Press, 1992). On the religious side the standard work of reference is M. Hengel, *Judaism and Hellenism* (London: SCM Press, 1974). The works of Grabbe and Hengel were each originally published in two volumes and later reissued in a one-volume form.

Abbreviations

AB	Anchor Bible
ABD	David Noel Freedman (ed.), *The Anchor Bible Dictionary* (New York: Doubleday, 1992)
AnBib	Analecta biblica
ANET	James B. Pritchard (ed.), *Ancient Near Eastern Texts Relating to the Old Testament* (Princeton: Princeton University Press, 1950)
APOT	R.H. Charles (ed.) *Apocrypha and Pseudepigrapha of the Old Testament in English* (2 vols.; Oxford: Clarendon Press, 1913)
AV	Authorized Version
BBB	Bonner biblische Beiträge
BEATAJ	Beiträge zur Erforschung des Alten Testaments und des antiken Judentums
BETL	Bibliotheca ephemeridum theologicarum lovaniensium
BJS	Brown Judaic Studies
BZAW	Beihefte zur *ZAW*
BZNW	Beihefte zur *ZNW*
CBQ	*Catholic Biblical Quarterly*
DJD	Discoveries in the Judaean Desert
ExpTim	*Expository Times*
GCT	Gender, Culture, Theory
JAOS	*Journal of the American Oriental Society*
JSOT	*Journal for the Study of the Old Testament*
JSOTSup	*Journal for the Study of the Old Testament, Supplement Series*
JSP	*Journal for the Study of the Pseudepigrapha*
JSPSup	*Journal for the Study of the Pseudepigrapha, Supplement Series*
JTS	*Journal of Theological Studies*
NAB	*New American Bible*
NIV	New International Version

NRSV	New Revised Standard Version
RB	*Revue biblique*
REB	Revised English Bible
RSR	*Recherches de science religieuse*
RSV	Revised Standard Version
RV	Revised Version
SBLDS	SBL Dissertation Series
SBLMS	SBL Monograph Series
STDJ	Studies on the Texts of the Desert of Judah
VT	*Vetus Testamentum*
VTSup	*Vetus Testamentum*, Supplements
ZAW	*Zeitschrift für die alttestamentliche Wissenschaft*

1

INTRODUCTION

The author and readers of a Guide such as this will find that the problems presented to us by the book variously known as Ecclesiasticus, or as the Wisdom of Jesus Son of Sirach, or as Ben Sira, are somewhat different from those associated with the books of the Hebrew Bible or even with other books of the Apocrypha and Pseudepigrapha or those commonly described as 'intertestamental'. The apparently ambiguous status of our text, in what sense it is part of the Bible, is one issue that we must address.

Secondly, we have to decide how to refer to this book. We can say straightaway that 'Sirach' will be the short title normally used in this volume, in accordance with the headings of NRSV. I shall look more fully at the different titles in a moment.

Then, an explicit date is given in the Prologue (and the very existence of a Prologue differentiates this from virtually every other book in the biblical tradition, though we may compare Lk. 1.1-4), and scholars have for the most part, as we shall see in a later section of this chapter, been content to accept that date as reliable. The Prologue implies the existence of an identifiable author (or more strictly two authors: the author of the Prologue and his grandfather), which differentiates it at once from the Hebrew Bible and the Apocrypha, the author of none of whose other books we know. This claim is made in the strict sense of authorship; it need not be denied that, for example, many prophetic collections contain words going back to the prophets after whom they are named. But that is quite different from picturing those prophets as 'authors'. It is possible that a conscious claim to authorship, either by Sirach himself or by his grandson, is one of the indications that we are dealing with a work from the Hellenistic world (Mack 1989: 65). In that world it was customary to make an explicit claim to authorship in a way that was not characteristic of the Hebrew tradition. This issue of the possible interaction between these two traditions will occupy us a good deal in this book.

Sirach has some claim to be organized in a clear outline structure, though the extent of this is something we shall need to explore in more detail. Nevertheless, the possibility of such a structure renders it very different from a collection like Proverbs 10–31, with which in many respects it might readily be compared. And (though this is less commonly agreed) many scholars have found it possible to detect an underlying purpose bringing the work together as a whole.

On the other hand some problems arise here which are not found with other biblical books. There is first of all, as we have already seen, the variety of titles under which the book is known. Secondly, there are complications with regard to chapter and verse enumeration. Then, more seriously, difficulties arise as to its language, for it seems clear that the language in which it has been preserved and handed down in tradition (Greek) is not the language of original composition (Hebrew). Then, fourthly, problems arise relating to the setting of the book, both geographically and with reference to its place within the Judaism of its time. Of these issues, the first two can be dealt with in this Introduction, along with the questions of dating and canonicity. The others raise more difficult problems and will be considered in separate sections later, along with some of the other questions which naturally arise as we try to understand any piece of ancient religious literature.

Title

The book is commonly referred to by any one of three different names: Ecclesiasticus; the Wisdom of Jesus Son of Sirach; and Ben Sira. These are derived from Latin, Greek and Hebrew respectively. (Grabbe 1992 is usually a reliable guide, and will be referred to again, but here his description of Ecclesiasticus as the 'Greek title' of the book is misleading [p. 176].) With regard to the Hebrew, however, we should bear in mind that none of the surviving fragments includes the opening of the book; no Hebrew manuscript offers us anything earlier than 3.6 of the present book. We thus have no means of knowing whether there was an original Hebrew title, and what it may have been.

Outside the area of scholarly discussion, the name by which the book is most commonly known is probably Ecclesiasticus. This has been the usual title in those English translations which have included the Apocrypha. It should, of course, be differentiated from the book Qoheleth in the Hebrew Bible, usually called 'Ecclesiastes'. The titles of the two books, though confusingly similar, are probably unrelated; whether there is any link in contents is an issue to be considered later. Among modern scholars it has been suggested (Eissfeldt 1965: 596-97), that the two names represent a deliberate association of our text with Ecclesiastes, alongside which it was often read.

However that may be, 'Ecclesiasticus' apparently means the 'church book', and this is its Latin title, found, for example, in the Latin Bible, the Vulgate. The first use of this title is commonly (Box and Oesterley 1913; Oesterley 1953; Brockington 1961) attributed to the church father Cyprian (d. 258 CE). In his *Testimonia ad Quirinum* 2.1, Cyprian is endeavouring to show that Christ was the first-born and the wisdom of God, through whom all things were made. In this interest he first cites Proverbs 8, and then goes on to Sirach 24, which is attributed to the same author (Solomon) as Proverbs, and is referred to as 'Ecclesiasticus'. A sequence of quotations using the same title is found in *Testimonia* 3.110-12. We need not concern ourselves with the supposed Solomonic authorship, but the title 'Ecclesiasticus', as we have seen, became the normal way of referring to the book in the Christian tradition. The usual explanation is that it was the outstanding example of a 'church book', that is to say, of those books which were much used in church worship but not included within the more narrowly defined canon. On this criterion, however, it has also been noted that the available evidence suggests that the Wisdom of Solomon was actually more widely used and quoted than Ecclesiasticus. The sixth-century church father Isidore of Seville offers a somewhat different explanation. He included a discussion of Ecclesiasticus in his *Etymologies*. He noted that its author was known, though he wished to retain the Solomonic inspiration, and suggested that its title was due to the way in which the structure of the whole church and its religious concerns might be found set out there (Sect. 246). These different explanations are not necessarily incompatible with one another.

In recent times it has become more usual to refer to the book by either its Greek or its Hebrew name. As to the Greek: Sirach, or to give it its full title *Sophia Iesou huiou Sirach*, 'The Wisdom of Jesus Son of Sirach', is the form found in the Septuagint, and the alternative to Ecclesiasticus offered in English Versions such as NRSV or REB. The Greek language had rules about acceptable forms for terminating nouns, and so Sirach is simply a Greek version of the Hebrew name Sira'. In a similar way the Hebrew name of the (grand-)son of Sira', Yeshua^c, has been rendered into Greek as 'Jesus', a phenomenon familiar from the fact that the central character of the New Testament, who will also have been named Yeshua^c, is regularly referred to as Jesus.

We note that the writer of the Prologue claims that he was the grandson of Yeshua^c (Jesus). Yeshua^c himself is regularly referred to as 'Ben Sira', that is the Hebrew for 'son of Sira'', and Jewish usage normally refers to the book as 'The Book of Ben Sira'' (Skehan and Di Lella 1987: 3). Here we should have Hebrew usage in mind, in which 'son' can also stand for 'grandson'. It thus seems that Yeshua^c himself was most probably the grandson, rather than the son, of Sira'. That cannot be established with certainty, for the different languages offer widely different readings in the section (50.27) where the names are set out. As Skehan and Di Lella (1987: 556) express it, the best that can be offered is 'a mosaic of what they contain'. NRSV, taking the same view as their reconstruction, based on the best Hebrew manuscripts, offers (in the Greek form of the names) 'Jesus son of Eleazar son of Sirach'. There are variations in the Greek text at this point. The RV translation, completed before the discovery of the Hebrew text, has 'Sirach Eleazar', and this is still preferred by REB. (A further complication arises here from the fact that some Hebrew manuscripts and the Syriac tradition also introduce the name Simon or Simeon in 50.27: either as 'Simon son of Jesus' [Syriac], or as 'Jesus son of Simon' [Hebrew].) Certainty is impossible, but it is generally thought unlikely that the tradition here preserves reliable information and the point will not be taken further. The neatest explanation of these phenomena, and perhaps also the most probable, is that we have to do with five generations of one family: Sira'; his son Eleazar, about whom nothing is known save his name; Yeshua^c; an otherwise unknown and unnamed son; and the author of the Prologue, whose name is never mentioned.

That these figures were indeed all lineal descendants within one family seems to be universally accepted by modern scholars, though it is not at once clear why this should be so seldom questioned. In the book itself the language of 'father' and 'children' is very frequently used (cf., e.g., 3.1), and the assumption is usually made that this represents a teaching situation rather than different generations within one family. The possibility should therefore certainly not be excluded that the individuals we have mentioned are those who succeeded one another as teachers in the 'house of instruction' which is put forward as the setting

1. *Introduction* 17

for these teachings (51.23). Certainly the willingness of scholars to accept these names as those of genuine 'authors' forms an interesting contrast with the situation in other works which appear to claim specific authorship, for example, Daniel, 2 Peter, but which are almost universally regarded as pseudonymous.

In the present context, for want of other evidence, the claim concerning authorship will be accepted, and it seems quite likely that five generations of one family are being referred to, though we have no certain means of knowing whether the original Sira' was an individual or whether it was a family name. With this somewhat complicated pedigree, it is not surprising that the book is listed in English versions of the Bible under such a variety of titles. It is also worth bearing in mind that knowing the name of the 'real author' and his forbears is in itself little more than a curiosity; many modern literary studies have made clear that it is the 'implied author'—the background from which he emerged, the social and religious ideology which he took for granted—that is more important for our insight into a piece of writing. This is an issue to which we shall need to return as we consider the setting of the book.

Chapter and Verse Enumeration

We shall look below (Chapter 3) at the different versions of the book. Here we may simply note that they do not always match one another in their detailed division, and this has led to some confusion, particularly in the enumeration of individual verses. Ziegler's major edition of the Greek text for the Göttingen Septuagint (Ziegler 1980) laid down norms which are now coming to be generally followed, for example, by NRSV, and it is that classification which is used here. Older translations are liable to follow different patterns. Thus, for example, as early as ch. 2 RSV has 18 verses, NRSV only 17, treating vv. 17-18 of the earlier edition as one verse. Similar discrepancies occur throughout the book.

A further complication arises in places where the majority of translations apparently omit verses. Thus in ch. 1, vv. 5 and 7 have been transferred to the margin, not only by modern versions such as NRSV and REB, but also more than a century ago in the RV. These verses are found only in later and more expansive forms of the Greek text, commonly known as GII, which include some 300 cola not found in GI (Skehan and Di Lella 1987: 55-56). They do not represent one single, more elaborate manuscript, but embody a variety of text traditions. NRSV has frequent footnotes in the form 'Other ancient authorities add...', and this normally means a reference to the GII text.

One last complication arises from the fact that it is virtually certain that two sections, 30.25–33.13a and 33.13b–36.13, have been transposed in the Greek text so that they are out of order. The correct order has been preserved in the surviving Hebrew, as well as in the Latin and other versions. This 'great displacement', as it was described by Box and Oesterley (1913: 280), meant that in many older versions and commentaries references in this section are given in a somewhat confusing form. Thus, for example, the pericope found in NRSV as 31.1-4, dealing with the anxiety caused by wealth, is listed by Box and Oesterley as '31 (34) 1-4' and by Ziegler as '34 (31): 1–4' (1965).

These textual complications imply that it is even more than usually necessary here to issue and to take heed of the warning that references should not simply be followed without checking that they do indeed refer to the required passage. (A brief appendix, 'The English Versions', at the end of this present work sets out both the title given and the practice with regard to chapter and verse enumeration of the main English versions.)

We shall not in this Guide be greatly concerned with source-criticism in the sense that that discipline has been applied, for example, to the Pentateuch, but it is worth noting that those who have felt able to detect secondary sources within Sirach have most commonly found them in and around this section where the displacement has occurred. 36.1-22, for example, with its unusual form of a prayer, has often been regarded as secondary. But there is no agreement on the proper criteria to be applied in separating out material in this way, and so we shall not attempt to pursue that subject in detail. It is, of course, a different topic from the observation that some of the manuscripts contain added material agreed on all hands to be secondary. We should also be aware that ch. 51 poses particular problems, which we shall look at in the next chapter.

Date

The date claimed in the Prologue is very widely accepted. It refers to its author coming to Egypt in the 'thirty-eighth year of the reign of Euergetes'. This ruler is commonly identified as Ptolemy VII Physkon Euergetes II, who began to rule in 170, so his 'thirty-eighth year' would have been 132 BCE. The translation itself presumably took place a little later, for the Prologue refers to a stay of 'some time'. Hengel 1974: 131 suggested that the translation did not actually take place until after the death of Euergetes in 117 BCE, but we cannot be sure about this. In any case it seems that the main body of work can be dated c. 190–180 BCE,

1. Introduction

allowing 50 to 60 years for the lapse of two generations, though Williams argues for a slightly later date (c. 175 BCE) on the grounds of the likely ages of those concerned (1994: 564-65). Whatever its precise date may have been, the underlying assumption is that the work should be seen as a unity, written over a comparatively short period, though one must admit that positive grounds for such an assumption are not very strong. It has been argued (Gilbert 1984: 293) that the work underwent a series of redactions, with chs. 1–24 as the basis which was subsequently expanded, with 25.1–33.18, 33.19–42.14 and 42.15–49.16 as successive stages of expansion. But Gilbert himself admits that this is no more than hypothesis, and positive evidence to support such a reconstruction seems to be lacking. In any case it appears that Sirach is quite different from most of the prophetic collections in the Hebrew Bible, which are commonly held only to have reached their final form over a period of centuries. If a comparison between Sirach and prophetic books is thought inappropriate, we may note that it is usual also to suppose that the final form of Proverbs, a work whose form is much closer to Sirach, is the result of a long period of development.

There are two positive pointers to support the date proposed. First, it is very probable that the high-priest eulogized in ch. 50 was Simon/Simeon, who had died in 196, and the second-century date would fit very well with that. Secondly, there is no sign of the tensions which developed into outright war during the reign of Antiochus IV Epiphanes (175–164). No trace of the bitter conflicts alluded to in Daniel and vividly described in the books of Maccabees appears in Sirach. One possible exception to this might be noted: the allusions in 36.1-22 to the 'foreign nations' (v. 3), 'hostile rulers' (v. 12), and the plea for pity on Jerusalem (v. 18). This might suggest some of the underlying tensions which preceded the more open hostility of Antiochus IV's time, but this rather generalized xenophobia is not unusual in the Hebrew Bible tradition, and it would be unwise to read more than that into such a passage. We have in any case already noted that, for literary reasons, 36.1-22 has often been regarded as a later addition to the main body of the work.

It should nevertheless be borne in mind that, as far as dating is concerned, this kind of argument from silence is dangerous; and in any case for it to have any great weight it depends on the assumption that Sirach was a Jerusalemite (see Chapter 4). Nevertheless, to the best of my knowledge no scholar has developed a serious case for any alternative date for Sirach, and the usual dating will be followed here.

To establish an early second-century BCE dating is of more than conventional importance, for that century was a very important period in the history of Judaism. It was a period when the relation between Judaism and the cultural phenomenon usually described as Hellenism developed in important ways. Concern with the attitude of Sirach to the development of Hellenization is a theme that will run through much of this book. Our knowledge of the third century remains very fragmentary, but from the time of Sirach onwards we have a much fuller picture. This is thanks largely to the books of Maccabees and the writings of Josephus, but it is certainly of significance to be able to place Sirach and his grandson in that context.

One other point with regard to dating should be borne in mind; it leads on to our last consideration in this section. As we saw at the outset, this confidence about dating sets the study of Sirach apart from virtually every book in the canon of the Hebrew Bible, where dates often centuries apart are put forward with all seriousness as probable. Apart from modern scholarly differences, this assertion of a second century dating may have played a part in ensuring that Sirach could not be included within that canon, when the convention came to be established that a date before the time of Ezra (fifth or fourth century BCE) was the latest possibility for admission within the canon. This is clearly implied by Josephus, who in *Apion* 1.8 lists the books revered by the Jews. 'Five are the books of Moses', then other books were written under prophetic inspiration down to the time of King Artaxerxes of Persia, but 'from Artaxerxes to our own day, the detailed history has been written, but it has not been granted the same credibility as the earlier writings' (Bartlett 1985: 176). That reference is paralleled by 2 Esd. 14.45, which speaks of Ezra being told to 'make public' the 24 books which are clearly regarded as the constituents of the Hebrew Bible (Eissfeldt 1965: 563). On such an understanding Sirach's date would have excluded the book from consideration as canonical, though, as we shall see in this next section, it was not neglected in Jewish thought.

Canonicity

As we have just seen, Sirach has never formed part of the Hebrew Bible, but there are indications that in some quarters it was regarded as 'quasi-biblical'. Its inclusion in the Septuagint shows the reverence accorded to it in some Jewish groups, and it has also been argued that the particular form of the Hebrew manuscripts from the Cairo Genizah and from Qumran (see Chapter 3 for details of these) was that confined to biblical

1. *Introduction* 21

texts. The reference in the Mishnah to 'heretical books' (*m. Sanh.* 10.1; Danby 1933: 397), with a condemnation of those who read them, has often been taken as referring to Sirach (Beckwith 1985: 367). The corresponding Tractate in the Babylonian Talmud contains an extensive discussion (*b. Sanh.* 100b) on why 'it is also forbidden to read the book of Ben Sira', ending with the assertion by R. Joseph that 'we may expound the good things it contains' (Epstein 1935: 680-82). Epstein goes on to raise the question whether it may at some point have been included in some canonical lists. (It is interesting to note that the talmudic discussion then moves on to Song of Songs, about whose canonicity there was also debate.) Sirach is also quoted in the Talmud in the form 'It is written', a designation normally reserved for quotations of Scripture. (See *ABD*, VI, 934.) Nevertheless, despite these indications of regard for the book it seems never to have been the subject of detailed scrutiny as a possibly canonical text within Judaism.

Its position in the Christian tradition is more complex. Should the church confine its Scriptures to the 'Hebraica veritas' and limit its 'Old Testament' to works found in the Hebrew Bible? Or was the whole Septuagint tradition to be taken over and regarded as scriptural? These positions, represented classically by Jerome and Augustine, have divided Christians since the Protestant reformation. The Catholic tradition has regularly regarded Sirach as one of its 'Deutero-canonical' books, and it is found in all Bibles in the Catholic tradition. Protestants have relegated it to the Apocrypha, and it is therefore excluded from many Bibles produced in that tradition (thus still, for example, NIV). More recently, however, in many quarters a more relaxed attitude has developed, and Sirach and the other books of the Apocrypha are studied for what they can tell us of the world from which they arose, and such translations as REB and NRSV include the Apocrypha. Nevertheless the claims made by some scholars that the canon must be the basis of authority has led to continuing interest in the role of the apocryphal books; M. Gilbert, for example, has claimed (1987) that all the different primary forms of the book (Hebrew, Greek and Latin, in both their short and long forms) should be regarded as canonical and therefore inspired. The matter is further complicated, as we shall see in Chapter 3, by the discovery of Hebrew fragments of Sirach within a 'Psalms scroll' discovered among the Dead Sea Scrolls at Qumran. To pursue this issue of canonicity in any greater detail would, however, lead us to become involved in a larger debate, which would take us a long way from the study of Sirach.

Further Reading

Bartlett, J.R.
    1985   *Jews in the Hellenistic World* (Cambridge Commentaries on Writings of the Jewish and Christian World 200 BC to AD 200, 1; Part I; Cambridge: Cambridge University Press).

Beckwith, R.
    1985   *The Old Testament Canon of the New Testament Church* (London: SPCK).

Box, G.H., and W.O.E. Oesterley
    1913   'Sirach', in *APOT*, I, 268-517.

Brockington, L.H.
    1961   *A Critical Introduction to the Apocrypha* (Studies in Theology; London: Gerald Duckworth).

Danby, H.
    1933   *The Mishnah* (London: Oxford University Press).

Eissfeldt, O.
    1965   *The Old Testament: An Introduction* (trans. P.R. Ackroyd from the 3rd German edition; Oxford: Basil Blackwell).

Epstein, I.
    1935   *The Babylonian Talmud: Seder Nezikin*. II. *Sanhedrin* (ed. H. Freedman; London: Soncino Press).

Gilbert, M.
    1984   'Wisdom Literature', in M.E. Stone (ed.), *Jewish Writings of the Second Temple Period* (Assen: Van Gorcum): 283-301.
    1987   'L'Ecclésiastique: Quel texte? quelle autorité?', *RB* 94: 233-50.

Grabbe, L.L.
    1992   *Judaism from Cyrus to Hadrian*. I. *The Persian and Greek Periods* (Minneapolis: Fortress Press; reissued in a one-volume edition by London: SCM Press, 1994).

Hengel, M.
    1974   *Judaism and Hellenism* (2 vols.; London: SCM Press; later re-issued in a one-volume edition by London: SCM Press, 1981).

Mack, B.L.
    1989   'Sirach (Ecclesiasticus)', in B.W. Anderson (ed.), *The Books of the Bible*. II. *The Apocrypha and the New Testament* (New York: Charles Scribner's Sons): 65-86.

Oesterley, W.O.E.
    1953   *An Introduction to the Books of the Apocrypha* (London: SPCK; reprint of 1935 edition).

Skehan, P.W., and A.A. Di Lella
    1987   *The Wisdom of Ben Sira* (AB, 39; New York: Doubleday).

Williams, D.S.
    1994   'The Date of Ecclesiasticus', *VT* 44: 563-65.

Ziegler, J.
    1980   *Sapientia Iesu Filii Sirach* (Septuaginta: Vetus Testamentum Graecum, XII, 2; Göttingen: Vandenhoeck & Ruprecht, 2nd edn).

2

STRUCTURE AND CONTENTS

Sirach is a long book. In terms of pages of English translation it is exceeded in length in NRSV only by Psalms, Isaiah and Jeremiah. Before I go further in discussion of the various problems which scholarly research has isolated, it may therefore be helpful to consider the varied literary forms found in Sirach and then to attempt a brief outline of the structure of the book and its main contents.

Literary Forms

One absolutely basic formal distinction should always be borne in mind: that between on the one hand those forms of exhortation addressed to a human audience and on the other hymns and prayers addressed to God. Sirach provides many examples of each, within the rich variety of its contents and of the forms used: moral, cultic and ethical maxims, folk proverbs, psalms of praise and lament, theological and philosophical reflections, homiletic exhortations, and pointed observations about the life and customs of the day (*ABD*, VI, 939-40).

The most detailed attempt to analyse these forms more precisely took place as long ago as 1914, in the first flush of enthusiasm for form-critical studies. Baumgartner noted that the most commonly represented form in the book, particularly its first half, is the wisdom saying, often of proverbial character, and usually with two members:

> In the treasuries of wisdom are true sayings,
> but godliness is an abomination to a sinner (1.25).

This is very closely comparable to material from the book of Proverbs. Again, there are many comparisons, similes and other figures of speech which place Sirach firmly within the wisdom tradition.

More distinctive is the frequent use of hymnic motifs, both in short phrases and in the extended hymn of 42.15–43.33. Other forms reminiscent of the Psalms are to be found, but these are for the most part in sections of the book which must be regarded as marginal: the communal lament in 36.1-21 may be a later addition; and 51.1-12, where a song of thanksgiving is found, functions as a kind of appendix to the book. But there are lament motifs in the main body of the text (e.g. 14.17-19). The 'woe' passages such as 2.12-14 are comparable with similar forms found in the prophets, and such a passage as 35.21-26 is also reminiscent of the eighth-century prophets, though here the likeness owes more to theme than to form. Baumgartner goes on to list some other forms (beatitude in 14.20-27; lament for the dead in 38.16-23), and ends his article (1914: 192) with somewhat dismissive comparisons, treating the use of many of these forms in Sirach as falling below the purity of their Hebrew Bible forms. We need not follow him in that judgment, which as we shall see later was characteristic of much of the scholarship of that period in its estimate of Second Temple Judaism. (Bergant 1997: 167 also provides a helpful, brief introduction to some of the form-critical features of the book.)

Structure

Scholars are sharply divided as to whether it is possible to detect an underlying, consciously intended structure in the Hebrew text. At one extreme Delcor claims that the book is no more than 'an unordered collection of sayings on very diverse subjects' (1989: 416), and Schürer in both the original and revised editions describes the book as an anthology (1986: 198-99). More recent scholarship has shown that such a description need not be as negative as one might suppose. We are liable to think of an anthology as no more than a gathering of other people's thoughts and ideas, but it has been suggested that a *style anthologique* may have been deliberately cultivated as a means of showing an author's familiarity with his literary tradition—in this case, of course, the texts that we know as the Hebrew Bible (Murphy 1996: 67). We shall look in more detail below (Chapters 7 and 8) at the way in which Sirach used this earlier material.

There have also been very different approaches to the structure of Sirach. The suggestion has been made (Gammie 1990) that it is possible to detect an acrostic structure within the Hebrew text whereby the themes of successive sections can be identified through successive initial

2. *Structure and Contents*

letters of the Hebrew alphabet: *ab* (father), *bosheth* (shame), *ga'on* (arrogance), and *da'ath* (knowledge). This is ingenious but perhaps rather farfetched, and it would certainly be unwise to put much weight on this suggestion. As we shall see in the next chapter, our knowledge of the Hebrew text is far from complete, and no other known examples survive of what Gammie proposed: an extended acrostic stretching over several chapters. A very sophisticated eye or ear would have been needed to detect it.

The most obvious division within the overall structure comes at 44.1, which is to the biblically-attuned general reader probably also its most famous verse. 'Let us now praise famous men' is the AV rendering, and it regularly features in church services of remembrance or commemoration. At this point NRSV has a sub-heading 'Hymn in Honour of our Ancestors', with the note that this heading is included in the Greek text. This division comes toward the end of the book, and the possibility should certainly be borne in mind that the hymn which follows is placed in this position as a deliberate climax to the book as a whole. If that is so, then clearly we should envisage an overall structure.

The sub-heading at 44.1 is, however, not the only one of its kind. There is a similar heading taken from the Greek text at 24.1, 'The Praise of Wisdom', and another, following the praise of the ancestors, at 51.1, 'Prayer of Jesus, Son of Sirach'. Another quite widely held view of the structure of the book is that ch. 24, rather than the praise of the ancestors, should be seen as its climax. It would perhaps be unwise to pursue this point much further, for to do so would take us into the realms of literary theory: how far are we as modern readers to be guided by the intentions of the original authors in discerning climaxes and particular structures?

For the sake of completeness we should notice at this point that there are other headings in the Greek text, but these do not seem to mark natural divisions in the same way as those just noted. In any case, without committing ourselves to any particular literary theory, it may be that the threefold division which a break at ch. 24 implies may be the best way to envisage the book as a whole. Though in some respects the following material is very close to that which has preceded, nevertheless the very specific identification of wisdom with the Torah which occurs in ch. 24 gives quite a different slant to a reader's perception of Wisdom in the following chapters. This remains true even if we take the praise of Wisdom in ch. 24 to be, like the hymn in 51.13-30, intended to round off the section which has preceded it, as some scholars have done. On the whole it seems better to stick with the division already indicated by the Greek text. So we have:

1–23	Wisdom and the Wise
24–43	The Meaning of Wisdom, with further reflection upon its application, and ending with a lengthy hymn on creation (42.15–43.33).
44–50.24	The Praise of the Ancestors

Even this apparently clear section poses problems: does the 'Praise of the Ancestors' end at 49.16, or should the eulogy on the high-priest Simon in 50.1-24 be included with it? The point is discussed more fully in Chapter 8 below. (Skehan and Di Lella [1987] take the view that 50.1-24 should be grouped with what precedes; those using their list of Contents [p. 5] should note that the reference to the Praise of the Ancestors ending at 50.21 is an error, corrected in the detailed commentary at p. 546.)

Preceding this, as we have noted already, a Prologue has been added; and there follows a brief epilogue (50.25-29), speakingly slightingly of Edomites, Philistines and Samaritans, and closing with a brief beatitude. This appears to have been intended to bring the book to an end, but there is then added a collection of psalm-like passages of praise and prayer (ch. 51). This last chapter is widely held to be an addition to the main body of the text, not least because of the disparate nature of its contents. Within this chapter, NRSV, but not REB, includes at 51.12 a poem found only in the Hebrew, and usually regarded as a later addition. Its repeated refrain, 'for his mercy endures forever', is reminiscent of Psalm 136, on which it appears to be modelled. Finally, there is added another poem, ostensibly in praise of wisdom, though with a strong element of self-praise, which is an acrostic in Hebrew (51.13-30). If, as some have argued, Sirach is consciously modelled on the book of Proverbs, this may be an imitation of the acrostic which brings the earlier book to an end (Prov. 31.10-31; Blenkinsopp 1995: 16). This poem is often regarded as autobiographical; if that is so, then the rather varied material in the last part of the book was presumably gathered by Sirach himself.

Contents

Within this overall structure the contents may now be set out in somewhat greater detail. One way of doing this is simply to set out the material found in chs. 1-43 in what seems to be a logical order of themes addressed, without concern for their order in the book itself (thus Skehan and Di Lella 1987: 4-5), and this has the advantage of bringing together different parts of the book in which the same theme is considered. Thus such issues as wealth and poverty, or the appropriate way of dealing with friends and family, are touched upon more than once, usually in extended thematic clusters, and it is helpful to have the different passages brought together for consideration. At least sometimes it looks as if the final editorial process was less precise than it might have been, and unnecessary repetitions and possible contradictions have been allowed.

There is, however, a sense in which this method of dealing with the material is a counsel of despair. It abandons any hope of discerning why the order in the book has been arrived at, and we are left simply with what modern scholars have deemed to be appropriate linkages. Others, therefore, either claim to detect a logic within the present order of the book, or at least consider that that should be the proper starting-point for our consideration. (Interestingly Di Lella, who in his larger commentary [1987] followed the method mentioned above, does offer an outline of the existing structure of the book in his contribution to *The New Jerome Biblical Commentary*, while admitting that 'there is little order in the presentation of topics' [1990: 497].)

This is indeed one of the major differences of opinion among those who have studied Sirach in detail. By comparison with other wisdom collections, notably the book of Proverbs, it is clear that the material is at one level much more organized. Proverbs, particularly in chs. 10-31, darts from one topic to another without obvious rhyme or reason (though many scholars have attempted to discern some logic in the ordering of its material), and each unit of two lines is usually self-contained; Sirach, by contrast, regularly devotes a number of verses to the great majority of the topics it is concerned with. This can be seen at a glance from the paragraph divisions in NRSV, which nearly always correspond to a specific theme. Thus, to take an example more or less at random, it is clear that the whole of 3.1-16 is devoted to proper respect for one's parents. In that sense Sirach is clearly more organized than is Proverbs.

But it remains doubtful how much further one can go, to justify a claim to detect any over-arching patterns in the arrangement of material. Thus 3.1-16 does not form part of any discernible larger whole, such as, for example, an exposition of the Ten Commandments.

Instead some of the themes raised here will recur again in other contexts (e.g. 7.27-28, which again counsels respect for parents, this time in the context of a more extended section dealing with family life [7.18-36]). We shall see also in Chapter 9 below, that Sirach's view of women, a topic on which strong opinions are expressed, is scattered through many sections of the book as a whole. It has been said, therefore, that Sirach 'had no clear plan for arranging the various subjects about which he wrote' (Di Lella 1990: 497).

It would therefore be quite a false quest to seek a continuous underlying plot holding the book together. Nevertheless, with all these reservations in mind, it may still be helpful to offer a brief sketch of the contents of the book. What follows owes much to the outline offered by Di Lella 1990.

The Prologue is written in Greek prose, and we shall therefore not expect to find anything corresponding to this when we look at the relation between the Hebrew and the Greek versions of the book at a later point. It is in effect an apologia for the translation that the author of the Prologue has undertaken, though its reference to the book as 'pertaining to instruction and wisdom' offers a useful clue as to what is to follow.

When we come to ch. 1 of the book itself this clue is immediately relevant. It is manifest from 1.1 that the basic theme is to be wisdom, its origin and the ways in which it is manifested, though we shall see that not all the topics touched upon seem particularly characteristic of the wisdom tradition. Nevertheless, the theme of wisdom constantly recurs. Here it is presented in the context of instructions comparable with those in Proverbs 1–9, as something to which human beings can aspire. We shall need to bear in mind that in some parts of the book wisdom is presented much more in terms of a gift of God beyond human reckoning, and this point will be explored more fully in Chapter 7 below. Frequently in these earlier chapters, however, it is made clear that the reflections are addressed to 'my child' (e.g. 2.1; 3.12, 17; 4.1; less frequently 'children', e.g. 3.1). (In fact Hebrew and Greek regularly use masculine forms; NRSV 'child/children' is part of its conscious policy of using inclusive language wherever possible. Compare REB and other more traditional versions, with their more literal renderings.)

As in Proverbs, and as we have already noted, it is very unlikely that these instructions should be confined to a family context; they are instruction or education in a larger sense. A characteristic feature is the imperative, usually in negative form as a prohibition ('Do not', often in series, e.g. 1.28-30). These warnings are interspersed with a series of maxims concerning good behaviour and further poems in praise of wisdom.

Di Lella describes Part 1 of the book as extending from 1.1 to 4.19. The divine roots of wisdom are stressed and wisdom is frequently referred to as 'the fear of the Lord' (ten times in 1.11-30, and often elsewhere). Yet it is also something which humans must strive for. Wisdom must be worked out in concern for one's parents, humble behaviour, and a proper awareness of one's social standing. Sirach was no revolutionary; the existing social order is regarded as sacrosanct.

Part 2 (4.11–6.17) is also concerned primarily with wisdom, but here there is greater emphasis on wisdom as warning against various forms of unacceptable behaviour: a whole series of 'Do not' instructions runs from 4.22 to 6.2. A properly balanced behaviour is required, with the tongue a particular threat to true wisdom. This section ends with aphorisms on the value of faithful friends.

In Part 3 (6.18–14.19) much of what has already been said is repeated. (One wonders whether the educational context of Sirach particularly lent itself to this technique of repeating the same themes in only very slightly different words.) So we once again find concern for honouring one's parents (7.27-28) and for true and false friendship (ch. 12). The outworking of wisdom in one's life is essentially prudential: 'Do not contend with the powerful... or quarrel with the rich' (8.1-2). We are rather a long way here from the prophetic tradition represented by such books as Amos.

Part 4 (14.20–23.27) begins, as have the preceding sections, with renewed praise of wisdom, and continues by spelling out in somewhat more theoretical terms the implications of true wisdom. Though its practical outworkings are not lost from sight, we find here more extended reflections on the divine power in creation (16.26; 17.1; 18.1 introduce such poems). It has been suggested that 15.11–18.14 should be seen as a distinctive unit within this larger section, beginning with a theodicy, refuting objections which blamed God for human weaknesses ('Do not say...'), and concluding with a call to repentance for human presumption. (Levison 1988: 34 discusses the unified nature of this section; the reference to '15.9' rather than to '15.11' in his sub-heading appears to be an error.)

It is within this larger 'Part' that we find the additional headings in the Greek text to which reference has already been made. They are reproduced in NRSV: 'Self-Control' at 18.30, 'Proverbial Sayings' at 20.27, and 'Discipline of the Tongue' at 23.7. Skehan and Di Lella 1987: 298 dismiss the second as 'an inappropriately placed gloss', and the third as 'hardly accurate'. However that may be, their presence does suggest the concern at an early stage to discern a structure within the work as a whole. It is possible, though it can scarcely be proved, that this relates in some way to the educational background of Sirach. In any case there is a difficulty in knowing how far the section thus headed is envisaged as extending. Perhaps, therefore, these headings should be seen as part of the history of interpretation of the book rather than as an integral part of the text.

Part 5 is taken to cover 24.1 to 33.18. It begins with the hymn in praise of wisdom, which may most appropriately be described as an aretalogy, a recital of wonderful characteristics, often in the context of the worship of a particular god or goddess. A number of such aretalogies in praise of the Egyptian goddess Isis have survived (Nickelsburg 1981: 60), an interesting comparison in view of the Egyptian links of Sirach. Some have seen the hymn in Sirach as in effect a 'retouched' Isis aretalogy. Knox was one of the first to bring out the similarities with Egyptian aretalogies, but he also detected a larger context; in his view 'the figure of Wisdom in Ecclesiasticus shows a startling affinity to a Syrian Astarte with features of Isis' (1937: 235). He felt that Sirach's presentation may be seen as a response to claims on behalf of 'orthodox Judaism'. He has been widely followed in this general understanding, though the expression 'orthodox Judaism' would now be regarded as somewhat anachronistic. (McKinlay 1996: 135-36 has a useful survey of views.) We need to bear in mind, however, that in the monotheistic Judaism of the second century BCE, wisdom is, of course, not formally regarded as divine, though it is nevertheless pictured in very elevated terms. This is an issue to which we shall need to return (see Chapters 7 and 10).

After this hymn the remainder of this section ranges widely, touching upon the dangers to wisdom. Most attention is paid to the threat to wisdom posed by women, a theme which dominates much of chs. 25–26, and one to which we shall return later (Chapter 9 below). But there are other dangers, associated with loose conversation and treacherous behaviour. The section ends on a more positive note, by spelling out the kind of life-style to which wisdom may lead.

Part 6, 33.19–38.23, begins by addressing itself to the leading members of the community, and it soon becomes clear that Sirach's audience were prosperous and well-established citizens. They were not themselves servants; their concerns were with how servants should be treated. To an even greater extent than in earlier sections, however, the impression given here is of a somewhat random association of themes, without any discernible guiding principle. It is within this section, as we have already noted, that the confusion between the Greek and Hebrew order of the text occurs.

Part 7, 38.24–43.33, by contrast, offers more extended treatment of specific themes. The section begins by praising the scribe and comparing his vocation very favourably with the work of other members of the community; and it ends (42.15–43.33) with a hymn in praise of God as creator. Only the middle portion is less clearly structured, beginning in a remarkably modern-sounding way with general reflections on the anxieties of human existence and ending with the familiar theme of the problems posed by daughters. The remainder of the book is taken up with the praise of the ancestors and the various appended sections that we have already noted.

It will be obvious enough that the division here set out is very far from self-evident, and it is only put forward in a heuristic way, as one means of organizing the material. Other commentators have discerned different groupings, but none of them would, it seems, claim that their method was the right or only possible way of structuring the book. Thus, by way of illustration, it is quite likely that for many students the other commentary most readily available in English will be Snaith 1974. He offers quite a different division of the book: 1.1–10.3, 'The Ways of Wisdom'; 10.4–18.29, 'Man's Life under Divine Providence'; 18.30–23.27, 'Maxims of Prudence and Self-Discipline'; 24.1–25.12, 'The Praise of Wisdom'; 25.13–34.8, 'Counsels upon Social Behaviour'; 34.13–36.17, 'True Piety and the Mercy of God'; 36.18–42.14, 'Man in Society'; and 42.15–43.33, 'The Wonders of Creation'. The structure of the remainder of the book is more straightforward. It will be noted that only at the end of ch. 23 does Snaith's division correspond with that of Di Lella. Both would probably agree that the structure they propose is no more than a useful means of dividing the somewhat unwieldy whole into more manageable portions.

Further Reading

Baumgartner, W.
    1914   'Die literarischen Gattungen in der Weisheit des Jesus Sirach', ZAW 24: 161-98.

Bergant, D.
: 1997 *Israel's Wisdom Literature: A Liberation-Critical Reading* (Minneapolis: Fortress Press).

Blenkinsopp, J.
: 1995 *Sage, Priest, Prophet: Religious and Intellectual Leadership in Ancient Israel* (Louisville, KY: Westminster/John Knox Press).

Delcor, M.
: 1989 'The Apocrypha and Pseudepigrapha of the Hellenistic Period', in W.D. Davies and L. Finkelstein (eds.), *The Cambridge History of Judaism*. II. *The Hellenistic Age* (Cambridge: Cambridge University Press): 409-50.

Di Lella, A.A.
: 1990 'Sirach', in R.E. Brown, J.A. Fitzmyer and R.E. Murphy (eds.), *The New Jerome Biblical Commentary* (London: Geoffrey Chapman): 496-509.

Gammie, J.G.
: 1990 'The Sage in Sirach', in J.G. Gammie and L.G. Perdue (eds.), *The Sage in Israel and the Ancient Near East* (Winona Lake, IN: Eisenbrauns): 355-72.

Knox, W.L
: 1937 'The Divine Wisdom', *JTS* 38: 230-37.

Levison, J.R.
: 1988 *Portraits of Adam in Early Judaism: From Sirach to 2 Baruch* (JSPSup, 1; Sheffield: JSOT Press).

McKinlay, J.E.
: 1996 *Gendering Wisdom the Host: Biblical Invitations to Eat and Drink* (JSOTSup, 216; GCT, 4; Sheffield: Sheffield Academic Press).

Murphy, R.E.
: 1996 *The Tree of Life: An Exploration of Biblical Wisdom Literature* (Grand Rapids: Eerdmans, 2nd edn).

Nickelsburg, G.W.E.
: 1981 *Jewish Literature between the Bible and the Mishnah* (London: SCM Press).

Schürer, E.
: 1986 *The History of the Jewish People in the Age of Jesus Christ*, III.i (eds. G. Vermes, F. Millar and M. Goodman; Edinburgh: T. & T. Clark).

Skehan P.W., and A.A. Di Lella
: 1987 *The Wisdom of Ben Sira* (AB, 39; New York: Doubleday).

Snaith, J.G.
: 1974 *Ecclesiasticus* (Cambridge Bible Commentary on the New English Bible; Cambridge: Cambridge University Press).

3

THE LANGUAGES OF THE BOOK

That the original language of composition was Hebrew is beyond serious question. This fact in itself invites brief comment. It is often stated that Aramaic replaced Hebrew as the normal language of the community in the Second Temple period, and certain parts of the Hebrew Bible from that period are written in Aramaic (e.g. Jer. 10.11; Dan. 2.4–7.28; Ezra 4.8–6.18). On the other hand it is noteworthy that all the biblical books begin in Hebrew. The use of Hebrew by Sirach may be seen as a deliberate placing of his work in the tradition of the Hebrew Bible. This need not necessarily imply that he consciously envisaged his work as being added to an emerging collection of sacred writings.

There are scattered references to the Hebrew text, and probably occasional quotations of it, in Jewish literature down to Saadia Gaon in the tenth century CE. In any case the Prologue of the book itself is largely a justification of the practice of translation of holy writings, and makes specific reference to the writer's own attempts to render 'what was originally expressed in Hebrew' into an acceptable form of Greek. To the best of my knowledge this statement, that the present form of the book represents a translation from Hebrew into Greek, has never been seriously challenged, even when doubts have been raised whether the Hebrew texts discovered during the last century reflect the 'original' text. And even if we did not possess the Prologue, in which this statement is specifically made, there is much in the book itself which betrays a Semitic original. For the most part it is good translation, but it is translation nonetheless.

The Hebrew Text

The larger commentaries all give an account of the discovery of Hebrew portions of the work (e.g. Skehan and Di Lella 1987: 51-62), and only the briefest of summaries need be offered here. The process of discovery began in 1896, when fragments originating from the Genizah (storeroom for no longer usable texts) of the Jewish synagogue at Cairo, in Egypt, were identified as part of Sirach. That period of scholarly activity resulted in the identification of four manuscripts (A–D) of the Hebrew text, which between them accounted for approximately two-thirds of the whole text. Though a few scholars at one time maintained that these Hebrew fragments were in fact a re-translation into Hebrew, either from Syriac or, by a very complex process, from the existing Greek, that opinion was not widely shared and has now been abandoned in the light of further, more recent discoveries. This general view does not, however, exclude the possibility that isolated verses or, on occasion, somewhat longer sections have been re-translated ('retroversions' is the term generally used) from Greek or Syriac into Hebrew. Different views on this are expressed by Di Lella 1966, who favours the likelihood of a few such retroversions, particularly from the Syriac version, and Rüger 1970, who maintains that the somewhat different Hebrew of the different manuscripts explains the phenomena otherwise attributed to retroversion. It is doubtful whether the available evidence is sufficient to come to a definite decision on this somewhat recondite issue. (For the fullest readily available account of the early discoveries, see Box and Oesterley 1913: 271-80.)

One more Genizah fragment (E) was identified in 1931, and additional parts of MSS B and C in the late 1950s, but the next great breakthrough came in the 1960s, with the excavations in the area of the Dead Sea. Fragments of the Hebrew text were found among the Dead Sea Scrolls at Qumran (Caves 2 and 11) (Baillet, Milik and de Vaux 1962: 75-77), with 51.13-20, 30 included among other writings in what is usually referred to as the 'Psalms Scroll' of Cave 11 (11QPs^a) (Sanders 1965: 79-85). The juxtaposition of Sirach with other material which came to be regarded as biblical is an interesting consideration for those concerned with the development of a 'canon' of Scripture. How that scroll, which combines canonical psalms with a variety of other 'psalm-like' fragments, including our section from Sirach, should be understood, is a question on which Qumran scholars are sharply divided, and cannot be taken further here. (See Flint 1997 for full discussion.)

3. The Languages of the Book

In addition to these discoveries at Qumran itself a further portion, covering 39.27–43.30, with additional fragments extending as far as 44.17, was found not very far away, at Masada. Yadin, who was closely involved in the excavations which resulted in this latest discovery, was in no doubt as to its importance. The Masada material is the most ancient extant, and he claims that it is 'closest to—and is perhaps identical with—the original' (Yadin 1965: 11). (The plates in his book illustrate the manuscript very clearly and bring over the fragmentary nature of the material discovered.)

To complete the story of the textual discoveries, we should note that two further fragments from the Genizah material were discovered in 1982; Di Lella (Skehan and Di Lella, 1987: 52) has provisionally called this manuscript F, since it appears not to be an additional part of any of the known manuscripts.

Yadin's claims no doubt owed much to the excitement of the discovery, and we need not accept them in detail to recognize how the availability of Hebrew portions of Sirach has transformed the study of it. Though the quantity of additional material thus discovered is not large, it is of major significance on at least three counts. First, the Hebrew manuscripts are very much older than any of the Greek material which has survived, and this has important consequences in the field of textual criticism. Secondly, the very existence of this material in hitherto unknown locales confirmed the wide dissemination of the Hebrew text. Thirdly, new light has been shed on many passages of the book, a development which is of considerable significance for exegesis.

These additional discoveries enable us to place the Sirach tradition in a larger context, but it is also important to remember that they are quantitatively on a fairly small scale; 'fragments' is the right word to apply to them, and it is estimated that about 68% of the complete text is now available in Hebrew—not a large increase on the two-thirds of which Box and Oesterley spoke some 70 years earlier. It is a curious fact that several of the sections of the book which have attracted particular theological interest are not found in the surviving Hebrew. Not all would agree with Boccaccini in describing these differences between the Hebrew and Greek textual traditions as 'clear traces of successive Essene redactions' (1991: 77), though it is likely that the Hebrew text has received edifying 'improvements'. The passage following 51.12, found only in the Hebrew manuscript tradition, and printed by NRSV but not REB, would be a case in point.

It is obviously important to bear in mind the fragmentary nature of the Qumran evidence. If one takes ch. 24 as one example of a chapter missing from the Hebrew, it is possible that its use in christological reflections by Christian writers caused some problems in the Jewish tradition. But it is difficult to envisage that chapter simply being omitted from any text tradition, and it may well be that its absence, along with other, less controversial, gaps, from the surviving Hebrew manuscripts is due to nothing more than sheer chance. We may note that a proposed reconstruction of the Hebrew original of ch. 24 has been offered by Skehan 1979: 374, but it can, of course, be nothing more than a hypothetical proposal.

Not for nothing, therefore, does *ABD*, VI, 936 describe the textual criticism of Sirach as 'enormously complicated'. Just a few of those complications can now be considered. It should be borne in mind from the outset that the characteristics of the Hebrew tradition of the book which have been outlined present textual scholars with a problem somewhat different from that to which they are accustomed in the Hebrew Bible. There the overwhelming tradition is that represented by the Masoretic Text, and until the discovery of the Dead Sea Scrolls only the Samaritan Pentateuch offered a significantly different set of readings. Even the Scrolls, as has often been noted, are remarkably close to the Masoretic Text in a very large number of cases. With the Hebrew of Sirach, however, we encounter problems perhaps more analogous to the Greek of the New Testament, where a choice often has to be made between rival manuscripts.

One other point about the Hebrew of our book should be noted. The quality of the language has been very variously estimated. It has been characterized both as 'beautiful classical Hebrew poetry' (Lang 1983: 148), and as 'hideous and late' (Di Lella 1966: 149). Such a diversity of judgment between competent scholars warns us that assessments of style inevitably contain a subjective element; it is perhaps also fair in this case to say that each judgment is exaggerated. One explanation of the character of the Hebrew, as we have seen, might be to suggest that it was actually 'translation Hebrew', a retroversion from another language, but the likelihood of such an explanation seems slight.

The differing characterizations may also owe something to certain underlying assumptions about the 'quality' of a language which need careful recognition. 'Classical' Hebrew is regarded as being that of the monarchical period, and to that extent Lang's judgment is surely misleading; whatever the origin of Sirach it was not earlier than the second century BCE and the language had undoubtedly changed from the classical modes of expression by that time. On the other hand it appears that for Di Lella 'late' is of itself a derogatory description, naturally paired with 'hideous'. It would be better to recognize that languages change and develop, and to take the Hebrew of Sirach as representing one stage in the development of Hebrew rather than be critical of it for not being something it never aspired to be. To engage in detailed consideration of such issues would take us too far from our concerns in this Guide.

It will be a matter of regret for English-speaking readers that no recent edition of the Hebrew text with an introduction in English has been published. Many of its problems are discussed in Di Lella 1966, which does not include the complete text, but the main working editions are accompanied by introductions and comments in Italian (Vattioni 1968) or modern Hebrew (Ben-Hayyim 1973). Still useful is the small volume by Lévi originally published in 1904 and reprinted in 1951.

The Greek Text and Other Translations

There are some complications also in the Greek text. This, as briefly noted already, exists in two major recensions: one thought by some scholars to be in essence the translation referred to in the Prologue, the other an expanded version, probably in part at least independently translated from Hebrew. These are commonly referred to as GI and GII. The verse division of the whole book, which dates back to the Middle Ages, takes both into account, but as we noted in our introductory chapter, most modern translations regard verses or parts of verses found only in GII as additional to the base text and consign them to the margin. (For detailed presentation and analysis of the Greek textual evidence, see Ziegler 1965.) The elaborations are generally of a 'reverential' character (Gammie 1990). In addition to these developments it has also been widely held that part or the whole of ch. 51 is a later addition. (NRSV notes some of the variation here between Hebrew and Greek texts, but it is necessary to consult the larger commentaries for detailed discussion of this topic.) The GII version is also reflected in the Old Latin, which at times reflects a different (and perhaps superior) order of sections from those in the Greek versions. No new translation was undertaken by Jerome when he embarked on the version which came to be known as the Vulgate, and so the present form of the book to be found in the Vulgate is essentially the Old Latin.

There is also a Syriac version, probably translated from Hebrew in or around the fourth century CE, and upon occasion its readings have been preferred to any other witnesses, though the quality of the translation has come under severe criticism. (Schürer 1986: 205; for fuller discussion of the Syriac version see Nelson 1988.) In addition to these versions, translations were also made into Coptic, Armenian and Ethiopic, but these languages are not accessible to me, and these versions are in any case generally regarded as being of only secondary significance for our understanding of Sirach in general and its text in particular.

It is not possible here to examine in detail the quite widespread use of Sirach made in later Jewish and Christian tradition. For the most part the quotations and allusions shed more light on the later period than on the text of Sirach itself. For a useful survey, see Schürer 1986: 205-208.

Textual Criticism

It might seem a natural question to ask, in the light of all this material, which text is the 'best', as providing a reliable basis for more detailed study of the work. Those experienced in textual criticism will throw up their hands in horror at such an assumption: rarely indeed is it the case with any ancient text, where the original autograph will virtually never be available, that one manuscript can provide all the answers to the questions we wish to ask. Only brief consideration can be given here to this issue.

It would be natural to turn to the Hebrew, as the language in which the book was written, as our primary text. But nearly a third (including, as we have seen, some of those parts which are usually regarded as being of particular theological interest) has not survived in Hebrew. Nor was the text of Sirach subjected to the rigorous editorial process at the hands of the Masoretes which gives a distinctive character to the text of the Hebrew Bible itself. The fact that many of them were found in a Genizah, the synagogue storage place for unacceptable material, might mean that the surviving Hebrew texts were early recognized as being defective.

The Greek version is the one which has been handed down through most of the book's history, and still remains the natural starting-point if we are to obtain a view of the complete book. But, as we have just seen, there are two main Greek manuscript traditions, which from time to time display important differences from each other, and though GI is usually given preference there is nothing like agreement that this should automatically be so in every case. Finally there are the other translations, particularly those into Latin and Syriac. Each has been preserved in a Christian context; each may well have been reworked in that context. Modern scholarly procedures would regard any adjustment of a text to make it more acceptable to its users as deception, but to envisage it in that way would be quite anachronistic. We need only reflect for a moment on the use made of their material by different synoptic evangelists, or, in the Hebrew Bible, of Kings by Chronicles, to realize that such creative working of a received tradition was widely regarded as perfectly acceptable. We shall see below (Chapter 8), when looking at the 'Praise of the Ancestors', something of how Sirach fits into this pattern of fresh use of traditional material. This whole practice has attracted a good deal of scholarly attention in recent years. The name habitually applied to the outcome of such reworking of older material is 'Rewritten Bible'.

By way of postscript to this section we should perhaps note that the translations of the book found in all the major modern English-language versions of the Bible are based on the Greek text. (Commentaries, of course, follow the individual decisions of their authors or of the series of which they form part.) For the nineteenth-century RV, the oldest English translation likely to be of continuing value for the serious student, the Greek form was the only one then known. More recent translations have made varying use of the Hebrew, while still retaining the Greek as the basic version. It can often be instructive to compare NRSV with its parent version, RSV; the later form makes much more extensive use of the Hebrew text (and from time to time the Syriac). It is NRSV which is normally followed here.

Editions

Hebrew
Baillet, M., J.T. Milik, and R. de Vaux
   1962   *Les 'Petites Grottes' de Qumran* (DJD, 3; Oxford: Clarendon Press).

Ben-Hayyim, Z.
   1973   *The Book of Ben Sira: Text, Concordance and an Analysis of the Vocabulary* (Jerusalem: Academy of the Hebrew Language).

Lévi, I.
   1951   *The Hebrew Text of the Book of Ecclesiasticus* (Semitic Study Series, 3; Leiden: E.J. Brill [1904]).

Rüger, H.P.
    1970   *Text und Textform im hebräischen Sirach: Untersuchungen zur Textgeschichte und Textkritik der hebräischen Sirachfragmente aus der Kairoer Geniza* (BZAW, 112; Berlin: W. de Gruyter).

Sanders, J.A.
    1965   *The Psalms Scroll of Qumran Cave 11 (11QPs^a)* (DJD, 4; Oxford: Clarendon Press).

Vattioni, F.
    1968   *Ecclesiastico: Testo ebraico con apparato critico e versioni greca, latina e syriaca* (Naples: Istituto Orientali di Napoli).

Yadin, Y.
    1965   *The Ben Sira Scroll from Masada* (Jerusalem: Israel Exploration Society).

Greek

Ziegler, J.
    1980   *Sapientia Iesu Filii Sirach* (Septuaginta: Vetus Testamentum Graecum, XII, 2; Göttingen: Vandenhoeck & Ruprecht, 2nd edn).

Syriac

Nelson, M.A.
    1988   *The Syriac Version of the Wisdom of Ben-Sira Compared to the Greek and Hebrew Materials* (SBLDS, 107; Atlanta: Scholars Press).

Further Reading

Boccaccini, G.
    1991   *Middle Judaism: Jewish Thought, 300 BCE to 200 CE* (Minneapolis: Fortress Press).

Box, G.H., and W.O.E. Oesterley
    1913   'Sirach', in *APOT*, I, 268-517.

Di Lella, A.A.
    1966   *The Hebrew Text of Sirach: A Text-Critical and Historical Study* (The Hague: Mouton).

Flint, P.W.
    1997   *The Dead Sea Psalms Scrolls and the Book of Psalms* (STDJ, 17; Leiden: E.J. Brill).

Gammie, J.G.
    1990   'The Sage in Sirach', in J.G. Gammie and L.G. Perdue (eds.), *The Sage in Israel and the Ancient Near East* (Winona Lake, IN: Eisenbrauns): 355-72.

Lang, B.
    1983   *Monotheism and the Prophetic Minority* (Social World of Biblical Antiquity Series, 1; Sheffield: Almond Press).

Schürer, E.
    1986   *The History of the Jewish People in the Age of Jesus Christ*, III.i (eds. G. Vermes, F. Millar and M. Goodman; Edinburgh: T. & T. Clark).

Skehan, P.W.
    1979   'Structures in Poems on Wisdom: Proverbs 8 and Sirach 24', *CBQ* 41: 365-79.
Skehan, P.W., and A.A. Di Lella
    1987   *The Wisdom of Ben Sira* (AB, 39; New York: Doubleday).

4

THE SOCIAL AND RELIGIOUS BACKGROUND OF SIRACH

It may seem to be a very drastic shift to move from considering the languages of the book to exploring its historical context. In fact, the move is less radical than it might seem. Sirach dates from the period when Judaism was finding its way in the encounter with the Hellenistic civilization which developed throughout the eastern Mediterranean world following the conquests of Alexander the Great in the late fourth century BCE. One of the concerns in that encounter was the issue of language, in a religious context in particular. Hebrew, the traditional language of Judaism, had largely given way to Aramaic in ordinary daily life. From the time of Alexander's conquests Greek was also becoming widespread. The question was bound to arise: Were the holy writings, handed down from earlier ages, to be preserved in Hebrew as a 'sacred language' accessible only to a learned elite? Or could they be translated into more accessible forms?

This issue of the proper language as a guarantee of the people's identity already makes itself felt in the Hebrew Bible (Neh. 13.23-24). We have noted already that though some late parts of that Bible are in Aramaic, its Hebrew component (always including the beginning of each book) is important. Sirach, as a scribe and a scholar, may have had a significant part to play in the preserving and handing down of the sacred traditions. We shall see (Chapter 6 below) that there is dispute as to the extent to which Sirach quoted earlier Scriptures, but his familiarity with them is very clear from the praise of the ancestors in chs. 44–49. Yet, as the Prologue shows, it was necessary to translate Sirach's own reflections on the Law and the Prophets into a language that would be more widely understood, while at the same time recognizing that such translation would alter 'not a little' the sense of the original.

4. The Social and Religious Background of Sirach

It is striking that it was for the needs of the Jewish community in Egypt that the author of the Prologue made the translation into Greek, for that is also the context of the most famous account of the translation of the Hebrew scriptures into Greek. *The Letter of Aristeas*, whose date is uncertain but may not be far removed from that of Sirach, is best known for its description of the seventy(-two) elders brought from Jerusalem by the king of Egypt, who after edifying court discussions are said to have produced a Greek translation of the books of the Law. The historical situation underlying that account is far from clear (Bartlett 1985: 16-17 provides a useful summary of the problems), but Aristeas offers an interesting parallel to the translation of Sirach and shows that this issue was a live one in at least one Jewish community of the Hellenistic world.

Second Temple Judaism

Before going further into detail, however, it may be helpful to give some consideration to the larger context of the period from which it emerged. First of all it is important to bear in mind that the study of Judaism in recent years has been characterized by increased attention to the Second Temple period. At one time it was largely neglected, so that it seemed as if the true 'biblical' period ended with the destruction of Solomon's temple, and what followed could be characterized as a decline. More recently there has been a great change of attitudes. More attention is paid to the later parts of the Hebrew Bible itself (e.g. Chronicles); the recognition of the Jewishness of Jesus of Nazareth has led New Testament scholars to enquire into what it meant to be a loyal Jew at the turn of the eras; more important still, what is sometimes called 'early Judaism' and sometimes 'middle Judaism' has been the subject of study as an important matter in its own right. Those concerned with Christian origins, those interested in the development of Judaism, and those studying ancient history without particular religious involvement have all explored this period.

Not surprisingly Sirach has had its full share of attention, not least because, as we have seen, it is one of the few writings which it is possible to date with fair confidence. One implication of what has been said in this section is that students should be aware of this revolution in scholarly attitudes. Where the texts themselves are concerned, older collections, such as *The Apocrypha and Pseudepigrapha of the Old Testament* (*APOT*), edited by R.H. Charles (1913), are still of great value, but care should be taken in using some of the older literature which often regarded this period as little more than an interlude, and often a rather deplorable interlude marked by the degeneration of the 'true' religion of earlier times, between the 'real' Old Testament and the time of Jesus of Nazareth.

It is important also to recognize another, and more recent, shift in scholarly perceptions. The older view was that the only legitimate response for Judaism was consciously to set itself over against Hellenism. The successors of Alexander who ruled Palestine, whether the Ptolemies in Egypt or the Seleucids in Antioch, were perceived as alien occupying powers. When in the 170s and early 160s the oppressive nature of their rule became intolerable, those Jews who were loyal to their ancestral traditions rose in rebellion, inspired by the courageous leadership of Judas Maccabaeus, threw off the Seleucid yoke, and gained their independence.

This is a powerfully evocative, but distinctly one-sided, picture, which owes much to two sources, one ancient, one modern. (We may notice also that some popular modern Israeli presentations liken the contemporary experience of their country to the time of the Maccabees fighting against alien forces which surround it, and this has occasionally helped to shape more scholarly attitudes in that quarter. It is not a topic that can be pursued here.) Reverting to the two sources of the picture I have sketched, on the one hand it reflects the ideology put forward in the book of 1 Maccabees. From a close reading of that book itself, however, it becomes clear that a substantial part of the population was content to live under Seleucid rule. We cannot here go into that question in detail, but it has come to be recognized in recent years that it is a gross over-simplification to envisage 'Judaism' and 'Hellenism' as two sharply opposed life-styles set over against one another in radical tension. For that reason it can give a false impression to speak of the events of Antiochus IV's reign as 'the Hellenistic crisis', as if this were a sudden cloud arising in a hitherto clear sky. This criticism can be levelled against the otherwise excellent account in Hayward 1996: 38-39, of the contribution of Sirach to our knowledge of the Jerusalem temple. (The standard discussion of this question is Hengel 1974, more briefly summarized in Hengel 1980; Grabbe 1992: 147-56 provides a useful 'Introduction and Bibliographical Guide'.)

A second, and much more recent, source for positing an antipathy between Judaism and Hellenism must also be noted. In the days of the 'Biblical Theology movement' (roughly the 1950s and early 1960s) great emphasis was placed upon the difference between Hebraic and Hellenistic modes of thought, with the Hebraic being strongly preferred as the truly 'biblical'. This approach came in for some extremely devastating criticism in the 1960s, and at a conscious level such readings are virtually extinct. (Perhaps the best-known exposition of this view was Boman 1960, with a powerful rebuttal by Barr 1961.) It may still be the case, however, that a suspicion of Hellenism, as somehow opposed to all that Judaism stood for, survives in scholarly discussion. It may have its influence in the understanding of Sirach.

Before we go further it may be helpful to remind ourselves that, despite the danger of making misleading comparisons between Hebraic and Hellenistic modes of thought, there are certain features of the 'Hellenistic world-view' which we should bear in mind. The Greek language is an obvious starting-point, as we have already noticed. But Hellenism encompassed a good deal more than language and its use in literature. Architecture, the cultivation of and respect for learning, and what may broadly be called 'life-styles' come into play. We can certainly observe that, whatever his opinion of these developments, Sirach certainly reflects them. One example would be his attitude towards doctors. In the religious tradition of Judaism they seem to have been regarded with great suspicion (2 Chron. 16.12), whereas they were generally given greater respect in the Hellenistic world. Sir. 38.1-15 reflects that more positive attitude.

With these general considerations in mind it becomes possible to consider more closely the social and religious background from which Sirach emerged. We may first consider its place of origin. The author of the Prologue speaks of coming to Egypt, with the apparent implication that he had moved from elsewhere. It would be natural to assume that his place of origin, and his grandfather's home, was Jerusalem.

The Geographical Setting

Outside the Prologue the nearest direct references to a particular geographical setting occur in ch. 50. They are twofold. First, and more generally, there is the picture of the high-priest Simon and the construction work that he had organized in and around the temple (50.1-4). Hayward (1996: 39) spells out the implications of this, in terms of the 'awe and respect' in which Sirach held the Zadokite priesthood in general and Simon in particular. He brings out some interesting differences of emphasis between the Hebrew of ch. 50, and its Greek translation, written at a time when the Zadokites no longer controlled the Jerusalem temple and for an Egyptian-based readership which certainly viewed the Jerusalem situation from a more detached standpoint.

All of this might certainly be held to support the Jerusalem origin of the book, though it is at best inference: the high-priest and the temple were venerated throughout Judaism, and it is not difficult to envisage Jews living in the diaspora as expressing their links with the homeland in the terms here set out.

More specific is the authorial note in 50.27. Greek and Hebrew texts show some diversity here, but NRSV has 'Jesus son of Eleazar son of Sirach of Jerusalem'. This would seem to be unambiguous, and many have read this as a clear indication that the author had been the head of a 'house of instruction' (see Chapter 5 below, on Sirach within Judaism) in Jerusalem. Against this, however, it can be argued that one is only known as coming from a particular place when one is away from that place. (One does not speak of X as 'a Londoner' if one is in London; only away from London does that become an appropriate description.) There is, moreover, some uncertainty as to the text at this point, so that the reference to Jerusalem has been regarded as an addition (Skehan and Di Lella 1987: 557).

There are some further points which can be made to support a Jerusalem background for the original form of the book. All our knowledge would lead us to suppose that the scrolls containing the traditions of the ancestors would have been more readily available in the precincts of the Jerusalem temple than elsewhere. Again, the kind of professional status enjoyed by Sirach seems also most readily to point to a Jerusalem context. Our knowledge of Jerusalem during the third century BCE, roughly the period of Ptolemaic rule, is very limited, but it is generally considered to have been a prosperous time, not least for the kind of professional classes represented by Sirach. The idealization of Simon in ch. 50 certainly has something of the feel of a hymn to the 'good old days'.

Nevertheless, it must be recognized that each of these pointers is ambiguous, and we should notice also his picture of the scribe as one who 'travels in foreign lands' (39.4). 38.24–39.11 have often been taken as a self-portrait (Marböck 1979) and, if this is so, the inference would be that he himself had travelled widely. The very possibility of such travel is significant as we consider the attitude of Sirach towards Hellenistic civilization. Such freedom and relative safety of movement would not have been possible in earlier ages. We may remember that

4. The Social and Religious Background of Sirach

Philo, the Jewish writer from the first century CE, was also an advocate of travel as broadening the mind (Jacob 1978: 251).

The journey to Egypt by the author of the Prologue is an illustration of this freedom of movement, and there are those who have held that the links with Egypt go back to Sirach himself. They maintain that the whole collection embodied in our present book took shape in Egypt. Some support for this view is offered by Sanders 1983, who draws detailed attention to the similarities between Sirach and various examples of Egyptian demotic wisdom. (The term 'demotic', originally applied to a simplification of the complex Egyptian script, in a form which developed around the seventh century BCE, has come to be applied more generally to the wisdom writings down to the turn of the eras. The discovery of the 'Rosetta Stone' in Napoleonic times proved to be the key to the decipherment of demotic, since it is inscribed in Greek and both hieroglyphs and demotic. It is a curious coincidence that the date of the Rosetta Stone, 196 BCE, is very close to that of Sirach.) While it is certainly possible that knowledge of this literature spread beyond Egypt, it is perhaps easier to envisage detailed knowledge of it being acquired in an Egyptian milieu. Thus Sanders draws attention to a number of links with the Egyptian Papyrus Insinger, whose original date is uncertain. It was once supposed that the work was actually later than Sirach, and so any dependence would have been from Sirach to Insinger, but it is now generally agreed that the original form of Insinger dates from early in the Ptolemaic period and thus precedes Sirach. In Sanders's view the words of Phibis, the implied author of the Insinger Papyrus, were directly used as a source by Sirach, and if this were so, it would at least raise the question of an Egyptian origin, not simply for the final translation, but for the main body of his work. There is no ground, it is argued, for supposing that the Insinger Papyrus would have been known in Palestine.

On the other hand, we should bear in mind that there is a good deal of evidence for supposing that wisdom texts and the themes they treated were widely disseminated in the ancient Near Eastern world. By way of parallel we may note that the nature of the links between the book of Proverbs, 22.17–24.22 and the Instruction of Amen-em-opet continues to be debated, but it seems clear that such links did exist. As long ago as 1929, Humbert drew attention to the association between a variety of Egyptian texts and those of Judaism. One of these, the 'satire of occupations' found in Sir. 38.24–39.11, I shall consider briefly in the next section. We may also note Sirach's concern with table manners (e.g. 31.12-14) as another issue frequently raised in Egyptian texts. In short, it may be that there was some kind of international currency of themes characteristically raised in texts of this kind, and it would be wrong to suppose that this offers very strong support for any particular place of composition. The variety of evidence just noted shows that it certainly cannot be proved that Jerusalem was the place of origin of the main body of the book, but it remains the most likely supposition, and is the assumption that will be followed here.

Sirach's Professional Status

Allusions have already been made to Sirach's professional status, and it is to that topic that we must now turn. Reference has just been made to the 'satire of occupations' in chs. 38–39, with its somewhat patronizing cameos of ploughman and artisan, smith and potter. The labouring classes are important for the welfare of society:

> Without them no city can be inhabited
> and wherever they live, they will not go hungry (38.32).

But it is equally clear that tradesmen of this kind would not be on the invitation-list for the author's next dinner party (and, as we have already seen, dinner parties played an important part in his social world [31.12–32.13]). They may indeed 'maintain the fabric of the world', but their limitations are obvious enough. This kind of picture has a well-known antecedent in the Egyptian 'Satire of the Trades', a frequently copied Egyptian text whose original probably dated back to the third millennium BCE, and may well have been a direct inspiration to Sirach. (An English translation is available in *ANET*, 432-34.)

The Egyptian 'Satire of the Trades' ends by glorifying the work of the scribes, and here it is followed by Sirach. The 'wisdom of the scribe' is to be highly esteemed, and he is to be granted the leisure he needs for proper reflection. 'Only one who has little business can become wise' (38.24), and this text has led Lang (1983: 148) to subtitle his treatment of our text as 'The Scholar as an "Honourable Idler": Jesus Sirach'. The attitude found in 2 Thess. 3.10, 'Anyone unwilling to work should not eat' is very distant here. To some extent this approach may be seen as an indication of an acceptance of Hellenistic values, which esteemed the life of honourable leisure, accompanied by study, as against the Jewish tradition which gave higher esteem to the life of action, and even manual work. (At a slightly later period the author of Acts draws special attention to Paul's work as a tentmaker: Acts 18.3.)

4. The Social and Religious Background of Sirach

Is it possible to be more precise in 'placing' Sirach? At the social level there is no difficulty in discerning where Sirach should be placed. The series of warnings in ch. 7 is particularly revealing. It shows that he must have been a landowner, one who had slaves to do any unpleasant tasks, very ready to look down on those less well provided for than himself, and regarding wealth very much as a sign of divine favour (14.3-19). Wealth must not be hoarded, but should be properly enjoyed. Blenkinsopp (1995: 17) provides a good sketch of Sirach's social position.

Some have regarded it as likely that Sirach was himself a priest. One Greek manuscript (Sinaiticus) describes him at 50.27 as *iereus o solumeites* (Ziegler 1980: 362; the same information is available in Rahlfs [1949: 468] for those who do not have access to the Göttingen Septuagint), and he is occasionally so described in later tradition, but this scarcely seems to be a primary tradition. The importance of maintaining the forms of worship laid down in the Torah is certainly stressed (e.g. 35.1-9). Again, the warnings in 7.4-7 against seeking undue honours have been understood (Hengel 1974: 133-34) as a reference to disputes between priestly groups with different genealogical claims, but it is doubtful whether so precise an understanding is required. More specifically, the role of Aaron and the other priests mentioned in the Torah is greatly stressed in the praise of the ancestors (45.6-25), and it is possible to see the eulogy of the high-priest Simon in ch. 50 as the climax of the book as a whole. But reverence for the priesthood and the priestly duties does not make one a priest, and there are no clear indications that Sirach was engaged in specifically priestly duties, though he may have been of a priestly family (Skehan and Di Lella 1987: 518). (It may also be relevant to offer the reminder that to speak of an individual Jew in the Second Temple period as 'being a priest' does not imply the regular performance of clerical duties in the way sometimes envisaged of the Christian clergy in our own time; priestly courses were set out by the Chronicler, but we have no means of knowing what proportion of those of priestly families were actually regularly engaged in such duties.)

Similar comments can be made with regard to the praise of the magistrate found in 10.1-5. Clearly Sirach greatly valued the role played by magistrates as they maintained the stable structure of society, but it is more likely that this was due to the way in which this facilitated his own scribal position than that he was himself a magistrate. We may be content to see Sirach as a scribe, provided that we remember not to give that description any of the unflattering associations which it often has both in biblical usage (Coggins 1990: 616) and elsewhere in the ancient world. The description of the scribe in the Chester Beatty papyrus from the New Kingdom, 'Be a scribe that your limbs may be smooth and your hands languid, that you may go out dressed in white, being exalted so that courtiers salute you' (Williams 1972: 218), offers an interesting mixture of irony and envy. We should understand then that Sirach was certainly no mere 'pen-pusher', a copier of earlier texts. To put it more positively, the scribal role went closely together with creative reflection upon the tradition and a concern to teach it to others.

Sirach and Hellenism

The more general issue for our present concern is the place of Sirach with regard to Hellenism. We shall not be surprised to discover that in this area scholars are divided. Hengel 1974: 138 quotes R. Smend, Sr, in a work of 1907 as calling Sirach 'a Jewish declaration of war against Hellenism'. Similarly some more recent scholars (Tcherikover, Nickelsburg) have regarded Sirach as a conservative opponent of Hellenistic tendencies. The emphasis on the Torah and on the sacred history of a special people, it is argued, naturally brings with it a distrust of the modernizing tendencies of Hellenism. Such a reading will lay emphasis on passages like 41.5-10, understood as a bitter condemnation of all those who have flirted with Hellenism. To do that is to 'forsake the law of the Most High God' (v. 8). A defence of the position which regards Sirach as wholly within Jewish tradition, unaffected by Hellenism save at the most superficial level, has been set out by Kieweler 1992. His particular concern, reflected in his subtitle, is to contest the views of Middendorp (see below, pp. 51-52), who saw the setting of Sirach as mediating between strict Judaism and Hellenism.

But the condemnations in passages like those just cited, though very bitter, are quite unspecific, and other scholars (Lang, Mack) have tried to probe below the surface of the text and note characteristics that may imply greater sympathy with Hellenism. For them the important features of Sirach are his reverence for learning and the general assumption of Hellenistic values. It is possible to hold, on this view, that he was trying to show how the best of the Hellenistic world was compatible with traditional Judaism. (I have the impression that those who take the former view habitually use the Hebrew form of our author's name, Ben Sira, while those who stress the Hellenistic links prefer the Greek form Sirach; but I have not devised any statistical test to establish this.)

4. *The Social and Religious Background of Sirach* 51

Part of our difficulty in judging his real attitude arises from the fact that any protest against Hellenism that he may have wished to make had to be expressed in the cautious and diplomatic language of the shrewd courtier.

An example of different approaches may be seen in the treatment of 14.18, which likens human destiny to

> abundant leaves on a spreading tree
> that sheds some and puts forth others,
> so are the generations of flesh and blood;
> one dies and another is born.

Skehan and Di Lella 1987: 260, commenting on this passage, cite five uses of the same imagery from the Hebrew Bible, and a number of examples of related usage. They end by noting that 'Homer employs a similar image', and a quotation from the *Iliad* (6.146-48) is offered:

> It is with the races of men as with the leaves of the trees; some, detached by the wind, cover the earth, while others, reproduced by the greening forests are reborn in the spring.

Lang seizes on this as a conscious allusion to Homer, and supposes that while it is possible that this is simply a matter of common usage, he regards it as much more likely that as an educated man Sirach would have been well read in Greek, citing 34.11-12 to show that he was thoroughly *au fait* with the Hellenistic world. Lang's attempt to provide an appropriate larger context is very helpful, though one must be doubtful whether the evidence will bear the weight put upon it.

Middendorp listed a very large number of possible parallels between Sirach and a variety of Greek texts. Each made use of an anthological principle to set out their preferred views. On this basis Middendorp attempted in his conclusions (1973: 173-74), to bring out a more nuanced view of the relation between Sirach and Hellenism. As is now widely recognized, there was strong Hellenistic influence both in Palestine at large and specifically in Jerusalem; the older view, of Palestinian and Hellenistic Judaism set over against one another, has rightly been abandoned, thanks largely to the work of Hengel. In Middendorp's view it was only one particular religious group, the *hasidim*, who resisted this influence. There is no evidence to link Sirach specifically with any particular political or religious party, Seleucid or Ptolemaic, but he may have been concerned that, if Jerusalem became a Greek polis, traditional Jewish authority and *mores* might be at risk. It is best, on this view, to see him in a mediating position between Jewish and Hellenistic traditions.

Middendorp concludes by noting that a fruitful line of comparison might be to note the links between Sirach and the Stoics. As with the Stoics, Sirach brings out strong links between the love of learning and its practical ethical working out in daily life.

This whole area is further discussed by Sanders. He notes the problems which arise from the fact that there is no Stoic literary evidence early enough to be a possible source for Sirach, so that a measure of speculation is inevitable in exploring this area. Nevertheless, following Hengel and others, he notes the oriental, and perhaps more specifically Semitic background of Stoicism. It is therefore proper to explore the possible relation a little more closely.

Sanders's method of doing so is by a critical analysis of the main article dealing with the subject, Pautrel 1963. Where Pautrel had found in 40.28,

> My child, do not lead the life of a beggar,
> it is better to die than to beg

dependence on Stoic attacks on the Cynics, Sanders supposes that this and many other alleged similarities with Stoic thought are better explained within the Hebrew tradition itself. He is similarly cautious concerning the other areas put forward by Pautrel as reflecting Stoic positions: 'human dignity, the unity of the world and the unity of humanity' (Sanders 1983: 51). In particular the eudaemonistic standpoint of the Jewish Wisdom literature is reflected in Sirach, and direct Stoic influence need not be postulated. One other passage sometimes cited in this connection (43.27: Hebrew *hu' hakkol*; NRSV, 'he is the all') is too brief to be more than an interesting point of comparison.

We may note in passing that this tendency to be sceptical with regard to supposed foreign influence is characteristic of much study of the Judaism of the last centuries BCE. Thus, for example, an earlier generation of scholars claimed to see widespread Zoroastrian influence in much of the literature of this period, whereas most of the supposed linkages are now more usually explained as internal Jewish developments.

This raises important questions for the topic we have been considering: the appropriate placement of Sirach in terms of Hellenistic culture more generally. Sanders, following Middendorp, though warning against exaggeration in the earlier work, makes much of suggested links between Sirach and the sixth-century Greek poet Theognis, who was much admired in the Hellenistic world. There are in fact considerable

4. *The Social and Religious Background of Sirach*

difficulties in establishing how much of what is attributed to him actually goes back to Theognis himself, but he wrote a series of brief elegies, reflecting on the world around him which he saw to be changing in disturbing ways. Like Sirach he regarded good breeding as essential, and found himself surrounded by what he regarded as vulgarity. Perhaps his best-known couplet is:

> Vain are the thoughts of men, and nothing our knowledge;
> but the gods direct all things according to their will.

This could almost have come from Sirach, save for the reference to 'gods', but the thoughts are so general that it seems doubtful whether we can make a strong case for direct dependence.

However that may be, his conclusion is that Sirach 'is entirely open to Hellenic thought *as long as it can be Judaized*' (Sanders 1983: 58; italics his), and that seems an appropriate conclusion. Sirach's concerns were with true wisdom and the fear of God, and he was not afraid to range widely in his search for ways of inculcating these essentials. His greatest debt was, of course, to the Jewish traditions of which he was an heir. But whereas a figure such as Judas Maccabaeus, at least as he is presented to us, vigorously rejected Hellenizing tendencies, Sirach's attitude was much more nuanced. It would be interesting, though well beyond our present concerns, to compare Sirach's attitude to Hellenism with that of the later figure of Philo, also a devout Jew who made full use of the resources of Hellenism in his exposition of his faith.

By way of postscript we may note a potential source of confusion in usage. Sanders's terminology includes both 'Hellenic' and 'Hellenistic', and the distinction between them in his usage is not always entirely clear. Save when quoting others the practice here will be to confine 'Hellenic' to Greece itself and in particular the literature of its classical period; 'Hellenistic' is a wider-ranging term, appropriate for the whole eastern Mediterranean world and beyond after the conquests of Alexander the Great.

Further Reading

Barr, J.
    1961   *The Semantics of Biblical Language* (Oxford: Oxford University Press).
Bartlett, J.R.
    1985   *Jews in the Hellenistic World* (Cambridge Commentaries on Writings of the Jewish and Christian World 200 BC to AD 200, 1; Part I; Cambridge: Cambridge University Press).

Blenkinsopp, J.
1995   *Sage, Priest, Prophet: Religious and Intellectual Leadership in Ancient Israel* (Louisville, KY: Westminster/John Knox Press).

Boman, T.
1960   *Hebrew Thought Compared with Greek* (London: SCM Press).

Coggins, R.J.
1990   'Scribes', in R.J. Coggins and J.L. Houlden (eds.), *A Dictionary of Biblical Interpretation* (London: SCM Press): 616.

Grabbe, L.L.
1992   *Judaism from Cyrus to Hadrian*. I. *The Persian and Greek Periods* (Minneapolis: Fortress Press).

Hayward, C.T.R.
1996   *The Jewish Temple: A Non-biblical Sourcebook* (London: Routledge).

Hengel, M.
1974   *Judaism and Hellenism* (2 vols.; London: SCM Press; later re-issued in a one-volume edition).
1980   *Jews, Greeks and Barbarians: Aspects of the Hellenization of Judaism in the Pre-Christian Period* (London: SCM Press).

Humbert, P.
1929   *Recherches sur les sources égyptiennes de la littérature sapientale d'Israël* (Neuchâtel: Secretariat de l'Université).

Jacob, E.
1978   'Wisdom and Religion in Sirach', in J.G. Gammie et al. (eds.), *Israelite Wisdom: Theological and Literary Essays in Honor of Samuel Terrien* (Missoula, MT: Scholars Press): 247-60.

Kieweler, H.V.
1992   *Ben Sira zwischen Judentum und Hellenismus: Eine Auseinandersetzung mit T. Middendorp* (BEATAJ, 30; Frankfurt: Lang).

Lang, B.
1983   *Monotheism and the Prophetic Minority* (Social World of Biblical Antiquity Series, 1; Sheffield: Almond Press).

Mack, B.L.
1989   'Sirach (Ecclesiasticus)', in B.W. Anderson (ed.), *The Books of the Bible II: The Apocrypha and the New Testament* (New York: Charles Scribner's Sons): 65-86.

Marböck, J.
1971   *Weisheit im Wandel* (BBB, 37; Bonn: Hanstein).
1979   'Sir.38,24-39,11: Der schriftgelehrte Weise. Ein Beitrag zu Gestalt und Werk Ben Siras', in M. Gilbert (ed.), *La Sagesse de l'Ancien Testament* (BETL, 51; Leuven: Peeters): 293-316.

Middendorp, Th.
1973   *Die Stellung Jesu ben Siras zwischen Judentum und Hellenismus* (Leiden: E.J. Brill).

Pautrel, R.
1963   'Ben Sira et le stoïcisme', *RSR* 51: 535-49.

Rahlfs, A. (ed.)
1949   *Septuaginta*. II. *Libri poetici et prophetici* (Stuttgart: Bibelanstalt, 3rd edn).

4. The Social and Religious Background of Sirach

Sanders, J.T.
1983   Ben Sira and Demotic Wisdom (SBLMS, 28; Chico, CA: Scholars Press).
Skehan, P.W., and A.A. Di Lella
1987   The Wisdom of Ben Sira (AB, 39; New York: Doubleday).
Tcherikover, V.
1959   Hellenistic Civilisation and the Jews (Philadelphia: Jewish Publication Society of America).
Williams, R.J.
1972   'Scribal Training in Ancient Egypt', *JAOS* 92.2: 214-21.
Ziegler, J. (ed.)
1980   Sapientia Iesu Filii Sirach (Septuaginta: Vetus Testamentum Graecum, XII, 2; Göttingen: Vandenhoeck & Ruprecht, 2nd edn).

5
SIRACH WITHIN JUDAISM

Whatever the nature of the relation between Sirach and the wider Hellenistic world it is clear that he greatly treasured his Jewish inheritance. This is made explicit by the references in the Prologue to the Torah and the Prophets, but also runs right through the book. The question immediately arises whether he thought of his own writing as comparable to those handed down from earlier ages which were now coming to be regarded as in some sense unique and authoritative. A related issue is the extent to which it is proper to speak here of a shift to conscious authorship, with intentional structure and composition, whereas earlier literature had for the most part reached its final form through a process of redaction of traditional material. At the very least the acknowledgment of authorship is a link with the Hellenistic world, where such claims were usual.

It may be that Sirach was content to be thought of as an epigonist, 'a gleaner following the grape-pickers' (33.16). The author of the Prologue clearly looks back upon the 'great teachings given to us through the Law and the Prophets' as something handed down from an earlier age, but it is not so easy to find specific references of this kind within the main body of the book. Two obvious exceptions are the allusions to various rivers in 24.25-27, which clearly embody deliberate reference to Gen. 2.11-14; and the praise of the ancestors in chs. 44–49, which is clearly dependent upon something closely akin to the Hebrew Bible in the form that it came later to be brought together. It is not surprising, therefore, that discussion concerning the development of the canon regularly regards Sirach as an important indication of a particular stage in that process; the idea of a canon is held to be established, even if it is not yet identifiable in later terms.

Sirach and the Parties within Judaism

We shall return in the next chapter to the issue of actual quotations within the book, but first we must consider the more general question of how we should place Sirach within the development of Judaism. Is it more appropriate to make comparisons with those who had preceded, particularly in the context of a developing wisdom tradition? Or should the stress rather be with the Judaism of the turn of the eras?

To attempt too precise an answer to this question would be unwise. The book, which, as we have seen, encompasses five generations, is first of all to be read for itself. Nevertheless, it would certainly be foolish to ignore the links of Sirach with the earlier traditions, and some of these will be considered more fully in the next two chapters. What about later developments? Though there are hints here of what would become clearer a century or so later, it does seem that it is when attempts are made to link Sirach more specifically with later Judaism that the greatest problems arise. First of all we should bear in mind the warning issued in many books by J. Neusner, that when considering the turn of the eras it is more appropriate to speak of 'Judaisms' than of 'Judaism', as if it were a single, definable entity. Again, while the New Testament and the Qumran scrolls provide some evidence from that later period, in each case there are internal ideological reasons which make the use of such evidence a delicate matter. Both the Jesus movement and the Qumran sectaries were opposed to and by influential groups within the spectrum of Judaism, and it is not at all easy to 'read' the situation in their day. And evidence from after 70 CE is widely regarded as suspect because of the passage of time and the traumatic events, in particular the Roman War and the destruction of Jerusalem, that had afflicted the community during that period.

In what may perhaps be seen as a negative way, Sirach can provide an important corrective to some misunderstandings of the Judaism of its period. An approach from the New Testament, for example, has often led to the supposition that Judaism was consumed with speculation about the coming and identity of a messianic figure. Such an interest in Sirach cannot be regarded as more than marginal. Though an article with the title 'Ben Sira et le messianisme' was published more than thirty years ago (Caquot 1966), its main thrust was to warn against seeing renewed royal hopes in Sirach, and the few Davidic references in the Praise of the Ancestors are set out much more in terms of thanksgiving for God's past mercies than in expectation of a future messiah

(Becker 1980: 83). Only in the passage found only in the Hebrew, and printed in NRSV following 51.12 (not in REB) does a verse like the following suggest a messianic hope:

> Give thanks to him who makes a horn to sprout for the house of David,
> for his mercy endures for ever.

It is widely held that this is one of the post-Sirach edifying improvements to which reference was made earlier.

If, of course, 'messianism' is given a broader meaning, as referring in effect to any form of future hope, then it is possible to see messianism in Sirach (Martin 1986: 152). 36.1-17 is a passage which clearly looks forward to a time when God will

> Give new signs, and work other wonders;
> make your hand and right arm glorious (vv. 6-7)

but no messianic figure is involved here, and in any case this passage is also widely regarded as later than the main body of the book. Again, the hope associated with Elijah in the Praise of the Ancestors that there will be a 'time to restore the tribes of Jacob' could only be described as a messianic expectation by stretching the definition of that term almost to breaking point. A more limited understanding, and a recognition that Sirach does not entertain messianic hopes, seems more satisfactory.

In the attempt to offer a more specific placing of Sirach in terms of what is known of the Judaism of a somewhat later period, there has been much discussion, particularly of the supposed relation between Sirach and the Sadducees and Pharisees. It is probably fair to say that this theme was more prominent earlier in this century, before the difficulties in using the later evidence had come to be recognized in the way that they now have, but speculation on such matters certainly continues. Box and Oesterley (1913: 282) developed an elaborate theory of a basic text of a Sadducean type, characterized by a central devotion to the Torah, and by the lack of reference to angels or to an after-life. They argued that this was developed, or perhaps deliberately modified, by additions described as 'fragments of the Wisdom of a Scribe of the Pharisees'.

Not surprisingly this ingenious theory has not been generally accepted. A basic problem is our ignorance of the characteristics and beliefs of the Sadducees, and the total non-survival of any literature from that source. All arguments proposing a Sadducean origin for Sirach, or any other literature, have to be purely speculative. As we noted in our previous section, it is possible that Sirach was himself a

5. Sirach within Judaism 59

priest, though that has to be a matter of inference for it is nowhere clearly stated. Even if it were so, it would be unwise to identify priesthood with the later views of the Sadducees.

There is one pointer which, if it could be given any historical weight, would appear to differentiate Sirach rather sharply from the Sadducees. According to the Babylonian Talmud the Sadducees differed from regular practice in allowing women to inherit along with male descendants (*b. B. Bat.* 115b). This would be so out of keeping with Sirach's dismissive attitude to women (see Chapter 9 below) as to show a clear difference. But the Talmudic evidence is of course very much later, and is itself shaped by a polemical stance which regarded everything Saducean as unacceptable, so that no weight can be put on it.

Secondly, there are difficulties with regard to dating. We can discern from the New Testament something of the activity and characteristics of both Pharisees and Sadducees in the first century CE, and Josephus enables us to date their origin somewhat earlier. But there is no real evidence to suggest that either group was already in existence as early as the time of Sirach, and we are in danger of serious anachronisms if we label him as a member of either group. (The use of terms like 'proto-Sadducee' is not helpful: either it is so generalized as to be meaningless, or it is more specific than the evidence permits.) Middendorp 1973: 174, saw some valid points of comparison between Sirach and the Sadducees, but concluded by rejecting any identification of Sirach as a Sadducee, and in this he was surely right.

Similarly various links between Sirach and the later Pharisees have been proposed, but again, apart from the danger of anachronism, these are too general to stand up to careful scrutiny. Thus, we note that Sirach shares with the Pharisees belief in angels (17.32), which should not necessarily be regarded as a later addition as it had to be on Box and Oesterley's view; an openness to the whole 'Scriptural' tradition; and, of course, a deep reverence for the Torah. But no Pharisee could have accepted Sirach's advice to 'eat what is set before you' (31.16); the food laws were, in the view of Pharisees, an essential part of the Torah.

It seems wise, therefore, to recognize and to give full weight to the fact that very important developments took place within Judaism between the time of Sirach and the turn of the eras, so that any attempt to read back our knowledge of the later period into Sirach's time is fraught with difficulties. Even so, this may be the most appropriate point to note such links as there are between Sirach and the New Testament, where the issue is, of course, complicated by the questions that arise as to the extent to which the New Testament can be understood as a witness to Judaism. Nevertheless it is interesting to notice that Sundberg 1964: 54-55 lists some 40 New Testament passages where a link with Sirach can legitimately be claimed. None of these make any explicit assertion that Sirach was regarded as 'scriptural', and it is striking that the greatest number of such allusions *pro rata* is to be found in the Gospel of Matthew and the Epistle of James, the 'Jewishness' of which has been much discussed. Certainly the same kind of prudential morality which characterizes much of Sirach is found also in James. By way of a sample of the kind of link that can be traced we may take one example from a different New Testament book: the command attributed to Jesus at Lk. 10.7, 'Do not move about from house to house'. This is certainly close to Sir. 29.24, 'It is a miserable life to go from house to house', but it seems much more likely to be a general prudential maxim than a specific quotation. If we look at links with Christian literature of the post-biblical period, as is done by Gilbert (1984: 300-301), the question arises whether such links are due to both Sirach and the later writings being products of a similar background, or whether the later writers are looking back on Sirach as a source of authority and inspiration, whether or not that should be described as 'canonical'. An exception to this general point emerges with the use made of Sir. 24.23, an issue to which we must return in our final chapter.

The various hints of links with later material noted in this section offer material for speculation, but little hard evidence, and it seems that the issue of the place of Sirach within Jewish tradition is better approached from the use made of earlier Jewish Scriptures, and it is that topic to which we must now turn.

Further Reading

Becker, J.
    1980   *Messianic Expectation in the Old Testament* (Edinburgh: T. & T. Clark).
Box G.H., and W.O.E. Oesterley
    1913   'Sirach', in *APOT*, I, 268-517.
Caquot, A.
    1966   'Ben Sira et le messianisme', *Semitica* 16: 43-68.
Gilbert, M.
    1984   'Wisdom Literature', in M.E. Stone (ed.), *Jewish Writings of the Second Temple Period* (Assen: Van Gorcum): 283-301.
Martin, J.D.
    1986   'Ben Sira—a Child of his Time', in J.D. Martin and P.R. Davies (eds.), *A Word in Season: Essays in Honour of William McKane* (JSOTSup, 42; Sheffield: JSOT Press): 141-61.

Middendorp, Th.
 1973 *Die Stellung Jesu ben Siras zwischen Judentum und Hellenismus* (Leiden: E.J. Brill).
Sundberg, A.C., Jr
 1964 *The Old Testament of the Early Church* (Harvard Theological Studies, 20; Cambridge, MA: Harvard University Press).

6
USE OF 'SCRIPTURE'

The Prologue begins with reference to 'the Law and the Prophets' and goes on to speak of Sirach himself (here of course the reference is to 'Jesus') as having 'devoted himself' to their study. It is not surprising, therefore, to discover that a good deal of attention has been directed to exploring the ways in which Sirach used 'scripture'. We need to bear in mind at the outset that there is a sense in which that term is anachronistic. It is most unlikely that there was a formal body of writings which could be called 'scripture' early in the second century BCE. But it is also clear that great authority was being accorded to many of those writings which came to form the Hebrew Bible, so the anachronism may perhaps be excused in the interests of convenience of reference. The author's self-reference as one who was 'like a gleaner following the grape-pickers' (33.16) is surely a reference to his position as a follower of those scribes who had set the Torah down in writing, and this at once implies a high regard for the sacred written traditions.

There is no doubt that general similarities, frequently of style and less often of wording, can be found to link Sirach with the wisdom tradition of the Hebrew Bible and especially Proverbs. Many scholars have drawn attention to this phenomenon, and those such as Heaton who regard Sirach as the inheritor of a long 'school' tradition, can suggest an obvious context in which these traditions will have been handed down.

Biblical Quotations in Sirach?

With regard to the specific issue of direct quotation, however, opinion has been more divided. A minimalist view was put forward by Snaith 1967, who rightly notes that the problem of identifying such quotations

6. Use of 'Scripture'

is greater than might at first sight appear. We really need first to decide what is the subject of our investigation: is it the Hebrew of Ben Sira, following the Hebrew Bible, or the Greek translation showing links with the Septuagint? Again, due allowance must be made for the possibility of editorial glosses. A more serious difficulty arises from our lack of knowledge of the literary, still less the popular, language of the Judaism of the period. What may seem to us somewhat unusual expressions in Sirach may do no more than reflect the idiom of the day.

With all this in mind Snaith concludes that the amount of conscious literary quotation from the Hebrew Bible is less than has often been supposed. He quotes Schechter and Taylor, who were among the first editors of the Hebrew fragments, and who described Sirach as 'a conscious imitator both of form and matter' (Schechter and Taylor 1899: 12), but his own view is that while there may frequently be allusion to the Hebrew Bible, conscious formulaic quotations are almost completely lacking. He notes the similarity between 42.15 and Job 15.17 ('What I have seen I will declare', both in the context of proclaiming the Lord's wisdom in creation) and other possible links with Job, but these are scarcely striking enough to establish clear dependence. As we have already noted, those passages which extol true wisdom as the fear of the Lord (e.g. 19.20; 24.23) have survived in the Greek versions only. For the greater part of the book, therefore, we can do little more than convey a general impression that its language and literary style are redolent of Scripture (Snaith 1967: 11). This applies also to such similarities as that noted by Dell, between the 'epilogue' to Ecclesiastes, with its view of human duty as fearing God and keeping his commandments (Eccl. 12.13), and the view of wisdom in Sirach (Dell 1994: 312). The concerns of Sir. 39.1-2, seeking out the wisdom of all the ancients, and preserving the sayings of the famous, are reminiscent of the despairing cry of the previous verse in Qoheleth that 'of making many books there is no end' (Eccl. 12.12). Another similarity with Ecclesiastes may be noted at 39.16, 'whatever [the Lord] commands will be done at the appointed time'. This is clearly reminiscent of Ecclesiastes 3, with its theme of appropriate times, and particularly of v. 11, '[God] has made everything suitable for its time'. Some will see in this a deliberate allusion of one work to the other; others may consider it no more than the kind of theological generalization characteristic of Hellenistic Judaism.

This of course raises two more general issues. First, we must ask how far the recognition of similarities of this kind is due to our knowledge of ancient Hebrew writing being almost entirely dependent on Scripture.

That question must here be left open; since so very little Jewish written material of a non-religious kind has survived, we have no means of knowing how far the Scriptures commanded a language of their own. Secondly, all discussion of the allusive way in which Sirach apparently used Scripture should be seen in the context of likely allusions to writings from other traditions. We have already seen possible links with Papyrus Insinger and other Hellenistic writings; it may well have been regarded as one mark of a truly cultured writer to be able to call his hearers' minds to other texts in this indirect way.

The section devoted to the 'Praise of the Ancestors' is of course consciously and explicitly dependent upon traditions which must surely have come to Sirach via what we should regard as the Hebrew Bible; the nature of dependence there is clearly different, and is dealt with in Chapter 8 below.

Even with regard to the main body of Sirach, however, other scholars have taken a radically different view from that of Snaith. Both Sheppard 1980 and Crenshaw 1981, writing independently of one another, engage in detailed investigation of the way in which Sirach uses the earlier literature. Sheppard wishes to use this evidence to support a particular hypothesis, and we shall consider this in a moment; here it is possible to note the more descriptive summary offered by Crenshaw (especially pp. 150-52). Thus he finds in 2.17 (so NRSV; 2.18 in Crenshaw's reference, following RSV),

> Let us fall into the hands of the Lord,
> but not into the hands of mortals;
> for equal to his majesty is his mercy

a direct quotation of 2 Sam. 24.14, where David had said

> 'let us fall into the hand of the Lord, for his mercy is great; but let me not fall into human hands'.

Even when one recognizes the warnings issued by Snaith and listed above, it still seems highly likely that this is more than an allusion and may indeed be a deliberate quotation.

Crenshaw goes on to refer to numerous passages which offer some kind of reference to biblical passages, the majority of those which he notes being found in Genesis. He argues that this is part of a conscious attempt by Sirach to see in the situation of his own community parallels with the experiences of the patriarchs, though our ignorance of the precise circumstances of Sirach's own time warn us against developing this argument too far.

A particular example of this re-use of Genesis material is offered by Levison, who detects in 15.9–18.14 (sic: surely read 15.11) an extended reflection upon Genesis 1–3. He sees particular themes and phrases from the creation story 'adapted and universalized' (1988: 41) to furnish illustrations of Sirach's understanding of humanity and its relation with God. Here clearly there is no question of direct quotation; instead we are in the much more subjective field of detecting allusions and possible cross-references. Some of the particular links that Levison detects may not seem convincing, but his general point, that Genesis is the background against which this part of Sirach should be read for its proper understanding, seems valid.

Sirach and Proverbs

More generally acknowledged are the literary links between Sirach and the book of Proverbs. Sanders 1983 devotes a whole section to Sirach's relation to Jewish tradition, and, following Middendorp, finds particular connections with Proverbs. Again we need to bear in mind that Snaith was primarily concerned with direct quotations, whereas Sanders ranges more widely. First of all he stresses similarities of form. Both Proverbs and Sirach begin with the praise of wisdom, and take care to identify that wisdom with the fear of the Lord. Thus, at Prov. 1.7 we have

> The fear of the Lord is the beginning of knowledge

with which we may compare Sir. 1.7

> To fear the Lord is the beginning of wisdom.

We shall see as we proceed that there may be significant differences in the understanding of wisdom in the two writers, but there should be no doubt as to the literary link.

It is, of course, essential to bear in mind another important difference between Proverbs and Sirach. It is commonplace in discussions of the Wisdom literature to note its lack of reference to the major themes which pervade other parts of the Hebrew Bible. Nowhere in Proverbs, for example, do we find mention of the Exodus and the Sinai covenant, or more generally of the requirements of the Torah. There can be no doubt that such concerns are very prominent in Sirach, and this should be borne in mind as we consider the literary connections between the two books.

Sanders draws attention to other such links. Both writers picture folly as bringing its own inevitable consequences, pictured in terms of falling into a self-dug pit (Prov. 26.27; Sir. 27.25-26); both point out that death is the inevitable end of the wicked (Prov. 24.19-20; Sir. 9.11). In more general terms we may conclude that the two writers share the same world-view. Indeed, this has been spelt out in detail by Gammie (1990: 359). He noted that both the author of Proverbs and Sirach function as advisers who stress the importance of piety, the need to conceal one's thoughts, and the ability to keep secrets. Self-control was important for each, particularly in avoiding adultery and in the care taken in one's choice of friends. If one was temperate, generous and kind, then the obvious underlying concern for success and good fortune would reap its reward. These themes are too detailed to offer references for each here, but they run through much of Sirach as they do in Proverbs. It may be that the description of Solomon at 47.17 as one whose 'songs, proverbs, parables and answers... astounded the nations' is intended to imply Solomon's authorship of Proverbs (Sheppard 1980: 14). One other much discussed link with Proverbs, the actual presentation of the figure of wisdom in the two books, will be considered in the next chapter, when we are looking at the more general issue of Sirach's relation to the wisdom tradition.

Other Biblical Links

Difficulties clearly arise at this point when we are considering direct dependence on the biblical tradition. As with the supposed similarities with the Stoics, already noted, we have to ask how far common membership of a particular tradition and a similar world-view can be claimed to amount to direct dependence. It is noteworthy that the relevant chapter of Sanders's book is called 'Ben Sira's Relation to Judaic Tradition'; he is rightly cautious about making more extended and specific claims as to dependence.

A greater degree of similarity between Sirach and the biblical tradition is detected by Gammie 1990. He observes how many links there are between the presentation of wisdom in Sirach and that in Proverbs, and these will be considered in more detail in the next chapter. But he also proposes similarities with Chronicles, noting how pride in the Jerusalem priesthood, and, perhaps more controversially, openness to foreigners, can be found in both writings. (This last point, of course, depends on the modern view which separates Chronicles from Ezra–Nehemiah. Ezra–Nehemiah would certainly not be regarded as showing the same degree of openness to foreigners.)

6. Use of 'Scripture'

As we have seen, another work which detects a conscious dependence on the Hebrew Bible is Sheppard 1980. In particular, Sheppard claims to identify a deliberate wisdom interpretation of a variety of material from the earlier tradition, particularly in his two 'case studies', which deal with chs. 24 and 16–17. In his view this may extend to direct reference, so that Sir. 24.23,

> This is the book of the covenant of the Most High God
> the law that Moses commanded us.

is a conscious link with Deut. 33.4:

> 'Moses charged us with the law,
> as a possession for the assembly of Jacob.'

He adds to this the suggestion that it is also possible to detect partial quotations, the use of key words, allusions to particular traditions, paraphrases of earlier texts, and a conscious use of 'biblical' metaphors in his chosen sections of Sirach (Sheppard 1980: 100-119). His larger contention, that wisdom provided a very wide-ranging category within which earlier traditions could be interpreted, is an issue which will concern us in our next chapter.

Before looking at that point in more detail, it may be appropriate to suggest that in Sirach we can see a precursor of the way in which material in the Hebrew Bible would be interpreted both in the Dead Sea Scrolls and in the New Testament. It is well known that in each of those bodies of texts, material from the Hebrew Bible was regarded as applying directly to the circumstances of the later community, whether it were those gathered at Qumran or the followers of Jesus. We lack the precise knowledge which would enable us to speak of a 'community' gathered around Sirach, but undoubtedly his message was addressed to those engaged in the search for true wisdom, and the earlier writings are here re-shaped as being applicable to that search. Thus the various spices described in Exodus 30 as brought together for the purpose of anointing the priests are understood in Sirach as part of the accoutrements of wisdom (cf. Sir. 24.15 with Exodus 30, esp. vv. 23 and 34). This 'creative' use of the earlier material may also be a pointer to the way in which Philo would interpret the Torah some 200 years after Sirach.

Finally in this section brief consideration should be given to the understanding of prophecy found in Sirach. We noted in our discussion of literary forms in Chapter 2 that Sirach made some use of prophetic genres. At the purely formal level these links are not extensive, but certainly some of the themes of the prophetic literature can be found in

Sirach. Thus 35.22-26 takes up the theme of God's impending judgment. At the same time, as we have also noted, Sirach's world-view seems to be very different from that of, for example, Amos.

There is one point where Sirach describes his own work as prophetic. The hymn in praise of wisdom in ch. 24 reaches a climax in an extended comparison (vv. 25-29) of wisdom with various great rivers—Tigris, Euphrates, Nile, as well as the other, less easily identifiable, rivers mentioned in Gen. 2.10-13 (Pishon, Gihon). This is then followed by a further comparison, likening his own authorial achievement to a life-giving canal (vv. 30-32), and he concludes by describing his own work as 'teaching like prophecy' (v. 33), which would be available for all future generations. It is striking that here prophecy is regarded as teaching rather than foretelling the future; something comparable with the 'Instruction in understanding and knowledge', which Sirach claims to have produced in his book (50.27), seems to be what is in mind.

When we consider 'the Prophets' more generally as a literary collection, it is clear that this formed an important part of the sacred tradition. This emerges from the Prologue, with its reference to 'the Law and the Prophets'; whether 'the Prophets' in this context is to be understood as substantially identical with the second part of the Tanak, in what came to be recognized as the threefold division of the Hebrew Bible, must remain doubtful. It may be that this was a general way of referring to those texts other than the Torah which were regarded as sacred (Barton 1986: 47). The specific references to prophets occur in the Praise of the Ancestors, and will be considered when we look at that in more detail (Chapter 8 below). We may simply note here that prophets were regarded in Sirach as figures from the past. Though, as we have just noted, he did claim prophetic status for his work at one point, there is no suggestion that he himself, or any of his contemporaries, was seized by prophetic inspiration. Indeed one suspects that such an outburst would have caused him great embarrassment.

We can summarize our considerations in this chapter by recognizing that, while direct quotation of the Hebrew Bible may be less characteristic of Sirach than has sometimes been assumed, he is still very much an heir of several of the traditions represented there, and developed them in his own distinctive but nevertheless loyal fashion.

Further Reading

Barton, J.
    1986   *Oracles of God: Perceptions of Ancient Prophecy in Israel after the Exile* (London: Darton, Longman & Todd).

Crenshaw, J.L.
    1981   *Old Testament Wisdom: An Introduction* (London: SCM Press).

Dell, K.J.
    1994   'Ecclesiastes as Wisdom', *VT* 44: 301-29.

Gammie, J.G.
    1990   'The Sage in Sirach', in J.G. Gammie and L.G. Perdue (eds.), *The Sage in Israel and the Ancient Near East* (Winona Lake, IN: Eisenbrauns): 355-72.

Hengel, M.
    1974   *Judaism and Hellenism* (2 vols.; London: SCM Press; later re-issued in a one-volume edition).

Levison, J.R.
    1988   *Portraits of Adam in Early Judaism: From Sirach to 2 Baruch* (JSPSup, 1; Sheffield: JSOT Press).

Sanders, J.T.
    1983   *Ben Sira and Demotic Wisdom* (SBLMS, 28; Chico, CA: Scholars Press).

Schechter, S., and C. Taylor
    1899   *The Wisdom of Ben Sira* (Cambridge: Cambridge University Press).

Sheppard, G.T.
    1980   *Wisdom as a Hermeneutical Construct: A Study in the Sapientalizing of the Old Testament* (BZAW, 151; Berlin: W. de Gruyter).

Snaith, J.G.
    1967   'Biblical Quotations in the Hebrew of Ecclesiasticus', *JTS* NS 18: 1-12.

7

SETTING: THE DEVELOPMENT OF THE WISDOM TRADITION

We have looked briefly at some of the links between Sirach and Proverbs. They have been further explored by a number of scholars, particularly in works dealing with the Hebrew wisdom tradition, so that, for example, Scott (1971: 201-12) could begin a helpful short treatment of Sirach by describing it as 'a latter-day Book of Proverbs'.

Three more general questions arise from these considerations. First, we may consider the kind of setting, or context, within which this tradition developed. Secondly, we must ask what kind of developments took place within the wisdom tradition. In particular, links with some of the apocalyptic texts have been proposed and these we must consider. Thirdly, the understanding of wisdom in Sirach has been seen as marking a significant theological development. We shall need to look briefly at texts such as Proverbs 8 and Job 28, with their distinctive presentation of wisdom, to gain a better understanding of the ways in which Sirach has developed the work of his predecessors.

A School Setting?

The reference in 51.23 to 'the house of instruction' has very commonly been taken as an indication of the setting from which the book emerged. The Hebrew manuscript from Qumran has *bet musar*, manuscript B has *bet midrash*. *Musar* is best translated as 'discipline'. *Midrash* is less easy to translate, but it is well known as referring both to the process of understanding and interpreting literary works, and to the outcome of such study. The term is found already in the Hebrew Bible in Chronicles (e.g. 2 Chron. 13.22, NRSV 'story') and *midrash*—in both senses of the term—played an important part in later Jewish interpretation. Here both *musar*

7. Setting: The Development of the Wisdom Tradition

and *midrash* are usually thought to imply some kind of wisdom school, the first which can be identified with fair confidence in the Jewish tradition

It has often been thought that schools existed earlier, particularly in connection with the transmission of the wisdom tradition (thus, for example, the article 'Education: Ancient Israel' in *ABD*, II, 305-12), but the evidence is at best oblique and such a conclusion has often been rejected. Thus for example Whybray (1974: 43) asserts that 'the evidence for the existence of schools with professional teachers in Israel, at any rate until late times, is not conclusive'. It is striking also that the immediately following article in *ABD*, II, 312-17 on 'Education: Greco-Roman Period' shares this sceptical view concerning the existence of Jewish schools in the period of the Hebrew Bible.

A much more positive, perhaps too optimistic, view of the evidence relating to schools is taken by Heaton 1994. We need not here concern ourselves with the scholarly differences insofar as they are specifically related to the Hebrew Bible. Whatever the earlier history, however, it is widely acknowledged that a school does provide a plausible context for Sirach. Indeed Heaton's first chapter is entitled 'A Jerusalem School Inspected', and he provides numerous quotations from the book to illustrate his basic hypothesis—that this school was dependent on a long educational tradition in Israel.

However that may be, it is noteworthy that Heaton regards it is as axiomatic that Sirach's school was in Jerusalem, and, as we have seen already (Chapter 4 above) this is the view which has usually been followed. We should in fact be unwise to lay undue stress on 51.23 taken by itself; it is a line in the middle of an acrostic poem, in which it is likely that all 22 letters of the Hebrew alphabet were used as the beginning of successive lines (51.13-30). This is scarcely the kind of context from which we should expect to draw factual information as to the context in which it is set.

Even if we are cautious with regard to this verse, however, there is much in Sirach that strongly suggests an educational or didactic context. Certainly the picture of the scribe in 38.34–39.11 makes best sense in a school setting. Similarly the 'you' who are addressed throughout the book are most readily understood as those whom the author wishes to lead or educate in the ways of wisdom. It might even be that the warnings against the 'inexperienced person' in 34.9-13 should be understood as a 'plug' for this one particular school against the rival claims of other academies, regarded as of lower quality. Rivalry between educational establishments is not a purely modern phenomenon.

Another point which we can only raise as a matter of speculation is whether this educational setting can usefully be linked with the development of the synagogue. Our knowledge of synagogues before the Common Era, particularly in Palestine, is extremely scanty. The picture of the activity of the scribe in ch. 39, and the way in which it envisages the assembly gathered for instruction in the sacred tradition and for worship, would fit in very well with what we know of the synagogue from a somewhat later period, but we can do no more than note the general congruity of such a picture. Our lack of knowledge does not allow any more specific identification.

There are numerous passages throughout the book that commentaries describe as 'didactic', whose concern seems clearly to teach those who need proper guidance. An example would be 33.7-13, beginning with a question inviting the pupils' serious consideration, and ending with an appropriate maxim in which the answer is embedded. This raises the question of possible links between Sirach and what is known of ancient Jewish education more generally.

Perhaps more basic than these points is the fact that the author of the Prologue perceived his grandfather's concerns to be related to 'instruction'. This is NRSV's rendering of the Greek word *paideia*. REB has 'learning', and the word is often most appropriately translated as 'education'. It is a common word in Sirach, occurring nearly 40 times. Not only is it a clear indication of the educational concern of the book; it is also striking that it is frequently bracketed with *sophia*, 'wisdom', which is one of Sirach's key concerns. In a sense they provide an inclusio for the whole book, since we find *paideias kai sophias* at the beginning of the Prologue, and at the very end of the book, 51.23-25, they are juxtaposed once again. (Admittedly the word *sophia* does not occur in the Greek text of 51.25, but the point is made in the Hebrew text and the theme is certainly present.) I shall explore the place of wisdom in Sirach slightly more fully in the concluding chapter; alongside its links with the Torah we shall need to bear in mind how closely it was associated with education and learning.

Whether or not Sirach was a pioneer in the field of Jewish education, it was a tradition which developed richly in later centuries. It would be misleading to propose any direct connection with the rabbinic academies of later Judaism, but it may not be irrelevant to note

7. *Setting: The Development of the Wisdom Tradition* 73

that, like Sirach, they presuppose a strong educational concern as a vital part of their religious tradition.

Sirach and the Apocalyptic Tradition

Bearing all this in mind, it is appropriate to notice another important development in the Judaism of Sirach's time. Apocalypticism has been much discussed; its origins and its characteristics cause much dispute among scholars; but there is still a widespread perception that from around 200 BCE and on into the early part of the Common Era a type of literature emerged which can usefully be described as 'apocalyptic'. (Whether that word itself should be used only as an adjective qualifying some other noun, or whether it can be used by itself as a noun describing a type of literature, is another debated issue which need not occupy us here.)

The older view was that the apocalypses were a later development of prophecy, and that wisdom and apocalyptic were poles apart, in their literary form, their life-setting, and more generally in their understanding of the world. That view was famously challenged by von Rad who claimed that 'the real matrix from which apocalyptic literature originates ... is wisdom' (von Rad 1965: 306). Very few scholars have accepted von Rad's thesis without qualification, but it has had the effect of opening up an extensive debate. Not only have links between the apocalypses and what is sometimes described as 'mantic wisdom' been noted, but a connection with Sirach has been claimed by several scholars.

Apocalyptic writings have often been regarded as the outpourings of the excluded, those away from the seats of power who had no means of expressing their frustration other than by claiming that the present world order would soon be violently overthrown. If that were so, we should be a long way from Sirach, whose whole book breathes an atmosphere of comfortable establishment within the existing structures of society. But a number of recent writers have argued that apocalypticism can equally be a product of the established order. (So for example Cook 1996.) If that were so, the links between Sirach and apocalypticism might be much closer, in social context if not in literary form.

Such a link was proposed by Heaton as long ago as 1956 in another, non-technical, work which drew attention to the similarities of outlook between Sirach and the author of Daniel, which is widely regarded as one of the first major apocalyptic writings, and probably dates in its final form from perhaps 15 years after Sirach (Heaton 1956: 19-23). Among links between Sirach and Daniel, Heaton drew attention to the shared delight in the Torah and wisdom, and the similarities between Sirach's description of the scribe and the way in which Daniel is characterized. More generally it has been noted by several writers that apocalypticism is a *scribal* phenomenon, and that at once supplies a link with Sirach.

Comparisons of the kind adumbrated by Heaton have been developed in more recent writing. Thus Argall 1995 (not seen) has drawn extensive parallels between 1 Enoch and Sirach in terms of both literary characteristics and conceptual features, and a link by means of the figure of Enoch has also been noted by Martin. He observes (1986: 153) the special role that Enoch plays in the 'Praise of the Ancestors', which begins with Enoch rather than Adam (44.16) and ends with a further eulogy upon Enoch (49.14), even though Adam receives the last word (v. 16). Martin notes other links between Sirach and the apocalypses through their common concern with history and with the importance of order within creation and the nature of the various threats posed to that order. (I shall look at this point concerning creation in the final chapter, dealing with theological themes.)

Davies 1989: 263-64 also draws attention to the prominence accorded to Enoch by Sirach, and comments further on Sirach's 'preoccupation with understanding hidden things', exemplified in the description of the scribal role in 39.1-11. Not all has already been revealed; it is incumbent on the scribe to 'meditate on his [the Lord's] mysteries' (39.7).

A comparison between wisdom and the apocalypses is also found in Boccaccini, and here it is placed in the larger context of a study of 'Middle Judaism', his perhaps rather confusing designation of the thought of the period from 300 BCE to 200 CE. It is noteworthy that Boccaccini entitles the relevant chapter of his work, 'Ben Sira, Qohelet and Apocalyptic: a Turning Point in the History of Jewish Thought' (1991: 77). This again illustrates a concern to bring together writings using motifs which have often been treated in isolation. For Boccaccini, Sirach represents an attempt to harmonize the concerns of the wisdom movement with the challenge presented by the early apocalypses. For him, 'behind the calm and asystematic style' of Sirach lies a 'bitter debate...and urgent questioning' (p. 80). Nevertheless we should bear in mind that the strong eschatological concerns characteristic of the apocalypses seem to be markedly lacking in Sirach.

7. *Setting: The Development of the Wisdom Tradition*

We shall need to return in the final chapter to the way in which Sirach draws together the previously distinct themes of wisdom and Torah. For the moment we may simply note that it is likely that comparisons between wisdom and apocalyptic will be more prominent in the discussion of the settings of the apocalypses than in that of Sirach. However that may be, they certainly serve to warn against the danger of dividing the Judaism of this period into rigid compartments.

The Figure of Wisdom

Wisdom in the Hebrew Bible, and especially the book of Proverbs, is often pictured as 'know-how', human ability to achieve one's objectives. That element is still present in Sirach. The series of comparisons in 21.15-28, for example, contrasts the intelligent person and the fool in terms of the wisdom shown in the behaviour of the former.

It is clear, however, that this is only part of the presentation of wisdom in Proverbs. As early as 1.20 wisdom is clearly personified as

> [she] cries out in the street;
> in the square she raises her voice

and in Proverbs 1–9 in particular there are numerous passages of this kind which present wisdom as a distinct entity. What is the appropriate language with which to describe such an entity? Within roughly the last half-century, there has been a good deal of scholarly debate on this issue. Particular attention has been directed to Proverbs 8, where it is very clear that wisdom is no mere matter of human ability. It is clear that wisdom can be said to be personified, but in part of this chapter more 'exalted' language is used of wisdom. A kind of self-portrait is offered, which sets out the role of wisdom in God's overall plan of creation (Prov. 8.22-31).

The modern debate on the understanding of this passage was inaugurated by Ringgren 1947, the subtitle of whose work contains the word 'Hypostatization'. Since then there has been vigorous debate whether such terminology is helpful to our understanding of the presentation of wisdom in Proverbs and also in Job 28. Was wisdom to be understood as in some sense a distinct personality acting as God's instrument, or even alongside God in creation? Or was the language here used that of poetic personification, which should not be given deeper significance? The much disputed translation of Prov. 8.30, where 'wisdom' has been understood as 'a master worker' (NRSV text), and thus in some sense acting independently, or as 'a little child' (NRSV footnote), and thus totally dependent on God, illustrates the problem.

In recent years an additional element has been introduced into this debate. Both the Hebrew word for wisdom, *chokmah*, and its Greek equivalent, *sophia*, are feminine nouns, and a number of scholars (mostly but certainly not exclusively women) have seen in this an important clue for a fuller understanding of divine activity in the Hebrew tradition. The concern is well expressed in the title of McKinlay 1996: *Gendering Wisdom the Host*. The role of 'woman wisdom' in creation has been discussed a good deal.

The relevance of these discussions for our understanding of Sirach will be obvious enough. McKinlay quotes Sirach in the very beginning of her study:

> Come to me, you who desire me,
> and eat your fill of my fruits (24.19).

At the very least it is clear that wisdom (the speaker here) is being personified, but as with the presentation in Proverbs, many have felt that the language here goes beyond a mere poetic figure. In particular, the links with an inner-Hebrew tradition represented by Proverbs 8 has led some scholars to question whether the proposed links with Egyptian aretalogies, mentioned in Chapter 2 above, are as important as has been claimed (McKinlay 1996: 135-36). We noted earlier that the tendency of earlier scholars to detect Zoroastrian influence within Judaism has largely been replaced by claims on behalf of inner-Jewish developments; something similar has been taking place here.

What is without parallel in the Hebrew Bible tradition is the dramatic development at Sirach 24. This reaches its climax at v. 23, where wisdom comes to be identified with the 'covenant of the Most High God', but such a denouement is not wholly unexpected within the terms of that chapter itself. Already at v. 10, wisdom claims that

> In the holy tent I ministered before him,
> and so I was established in Zion.

Such a claim is very different from anything in the earlier passages. In Job 28 it is the inaccessibility of wisdom which is stressed, and in Proverbs 8 there are no specific links with Israel's own traditions. Here, though wisdom held sway 'over every people and nation' (24.6), it was in the Torah, practised in Jerusalem, that she found her true home.

Such a striking claim as this differs from anything we know of in the earlier wisdom tradition. It may represent a mode of thinking that was

7. *Setting: The Development of the Wisdom Tradition* 77

developing more widely in the Judaism of Sirach's day, for similar ideas are found in Baruch 4. (This is a work whose date is much disputed, but it may not be far from that of Sirach.) We shall need to consider some of the theological implications of this development in the final chapter.

Further Reading

Argall, R.A.
    1995   *1 Enoch and Sirach: A Comparative Literary and Conceptual Analysis of the Themes of Revelation, Creation and Judgment* (SBL Early Judaism and its Literature, 8; Atlanta: Scholars Press).

Boccaccini, G.
    1991   *Middle Judaism: Jewish Thought, 300 BCE to 200 CE* (Minneapolis: Fortress Press).

Cook, S.L.
    1996   *Prophecy and Apocalypticism: The Postexilic Social Setting* (Minneapolis: Fortress Press).

Davies, P.R.
    1989   'The Social World of the Apocalyptic Writings', in R.E. Clements (ed.), *The World of Ancient Israel: Sociological, Anthropological and Political Perspectives* (Cambridge: Cambridge University Press): 251-71.

Heaton, E.W.
    1956   *The Book of Daniel* (Torch Commentary; London: SCM Press).
    1994   *The School Tradition of the Old Testament* (Oxford: Oxford University Press).

Martin, J.D.
    1986   'Ben Sira—a Child of his Time', in J.D. Martin and P.R. Davies (ed.), *A Word in Season: Essays in Honour of William McKane* (JSOTSup, 42; Sheffield: JSOT Press): 141-61.

McKinlay, J.E.
    1996   *Gendering Wisdom the Host: Biblical Invitations to Eat and Drink* (JSOTSup, 216; Sheffield: Sheffield Academic Press).

Rad, G. von
    1965   *Old Testament Theology, II* (trans. D.M.G. Stalker from the German edition of 1960; Edinburgh: Oliver & Boyd).

Ringgren, H.
    1947   *Word and Wisdom: Studies in the Hypostatization of Divine Qualities and Functions in the Ancient Near East* (Lund: Hakan Ohlssons Boktryckeri).

Scott, R.B.Y.
    1971   *The Way of Wisdom in the Old Testament* (New York: Macmillan).

Whybray, R.N.
    1974   *The Intellectual Tradition in the Old Testament* (BZAW, 135; Berlin: W. de Gruyter).

8

PRAISE OF THE ANCESTORS

One section of the book is so distinctive as to demand separate consideration. This is the 'Praise of the Ancestors' in chs. 44–49 or 50. It may seem curious to be uncertain of the extent of a section which begins so clearly, yet there is room for differences of judgment here. The recital of the praises of the people's ancestors seems to end at 49.16, and the reference there to 'Adam' makes it seem as if the author intended a form of inclusio, with the end matching the beginning. In fact, this is less clear than it might seem, for Adam is not mentioned at the beginning of the list. Various authors (e.g. Lee 1986) have therefore argued that the praise of Simon in ch. 50 is to be understood, not as a mere epilogue, or a separate part of the book, but as the climax to what has preceded. Certainly the placing of the eulogy on Simon is not accidental, whether or not it is seen as an integral part of the 'Praise of the Ancestors'.

A form found several times in the Hebrew Bible is the rehearsal of the people's history. Pss. 78; 105; 106; 135–136; and Neh. 9.6-37 are all examples of the genre, and it is continued in the New Testament in Acts 7 and Hebrews 11. But the examples from the Hebrew Bible in particular are confined to the early period of that history, either being limited to the period prior to the settlement in Canaan or at the most extending to David. (Nehemiah 9 does make later references, but the outline itself is confined to the early period.) Furthermore, the way in which they deal with the events they describe focuses very strongly on God's saving action. Here by contrast, though it was 'the Lord [who] apportioned to them great glory' (44.2), it is essentially human action which is the subject of praise. We may say, therefore, that though there are similarities with the other examples mentioned (perhaps somewhat overstated by Skehan and Di Lella 1987: 499-500), this section of Sirach stands as unique in the way it parades before us the great figures of Israel's past.

We should notice also the concern with individuals in Sirach, for this is in itself enough to make an important difference between this section and the other examples mentioned. Though particular individuals may be named (e.g. in Ps. 106.16-18), the earlier passages are to a much greater extent concerned with the people as a whole, whereas here named individuals are the focus of attention. There are comparable outlines focusing on individuals in Wis. 10.1–11.4 and in 1 Macc. 2.51-60, but each of these is later than Sirach (Martin 1986: 142-45). Indeed it has been suggested (Gammie 1990: 372) that it is more appropriate to look to other examples of Hellenistic rhetoric if we want parallels to this section.

As to the material contained within the Praise of the Ancestors, it is very doubtful whether any source other than the Hebrew Bible itself underlies these brief portraits. It is certainly true that particular details are not specifically mentioned in the biblical accounts, but these developments seem to be due more to poetic licence than to any conscious use of other literary sources. It should be borne in mind also that the example of freedom with the received text had already been set by, for example, the books of Chronicles, and is a characteristic feature of biblical interpretation at the turn of the eras. What is less clear is whether the listing of different types of admirable life set out in 44.3-6 is intended, as it were, to provide a 'table of contents' for what is to follow. More probable than such an explanation is the view that the categories there introduced are those which the author himself esteemed, and which he supposed in quite general terms would be illustrated by those he was about to list.

Arguments from silence are always risky, and never more so than in a case like this where an element of choice clearly underlies those who feature in the catalogue. Nevertheless it is worth noting that there are some striking omissions from the list which should be borne in mind. The most obvious omission is that of any women; there is no place here for figures such as Deborah or Ruth. This wholly male character of the list seems to be taken for granted by scholars; we shall look in the next chapter at Sirach's attitude to women.

Among males who might have been supposed to be eligible for inclusion we note that in ch. 49 the heroes at the time of the exile do not include Daniel alongside Jeremiah and Ezekiel, and this must be regarded as an additional pointer to the fact, well established on other grounds, of the late composition of the book of Daniel. In Sirach's time there were no doubt popular stories circulating of the exploits of Daniel and his friends, such as are now incorporated in Daniel 2–6, but the bringing together of the Daniel material into a collection which would become 'Scripture' took place at a later stage.

Another omission often regarded as significant is that of Ezra. Nehemiah is mentioned briefly (49.13), but not Ezra, a situation which has led to what has been described as 'a rash of proposals' (Soggin 1993: 292), though in fact Soggin mentions only two short articles. Indeed, some scholars (Garbini 1988: 152) and in an earlier generation Torrey 1970 (=1910) were led, partly by this omission, to question the very existence of Ezra. If this conclusion is thought to be too extreme, we are certainly invited to reflect whether Ezra's place in Second Temple Judaism may perhaps have been less significant than Ezra 7–10, Nehemiah 8 would lead us to suppose. Alternatively, it might be that there were tensions within the community around Sirach which led to the playing down of Ezra's role.

Turning now to those who *are* mentioned in the list, the doubts concerning the extent of Sirach's dependence on traditions enshrined in the Hebrew Bible are here largely removed. The dependence of this whole section on Scriptural traditions is well illustrated by the frequent use of key words and phrases from the canonical writings, though once again direct quotations are comparatively rare. Snaith offers a wide-ranging list of passages which appear to borrow at least some of their phraseology from the Hebrew Bible. It is striking that the characters who are highlighted—Snaith focuses upon Aaron, Samuel and Elijah as examples—are alluded to in differing parts of the Torah and Prophets: Exodus, 1 Samuel, 1 Kings, Malachi.

Recent studies of the literary phenomenon which has come to be known as 'Rewritten Bible' may provide us with some further insight into this material. (A brief introduction to this concept, with reference to this part of Sirach, is provided by Hayward 1990: 595-98.) While we need not doubt the author's interest and pride in the characters whose achievements he describes, it is also important to notice the way in which many of them illustrate particular concerns of Sirach. Thus, the praise of the 'patriarchs' in Genesis is held together by reference to them as the recipients of the covenants (44.18, 20, 22; cf. also 45.24-25). The importance of priesthood for the author is emphasized by the very extended treatment afforded to Aaron (45.6-22), and to Phinehas, a

8. Praise of the Ancestors

figure with only one primary reference in the Hebrew Bible (Num. 25; there are a few other less direct references in Numbers and Joshua), but one who is singled out in various retellings of the people's past. Thus we have 45.23-25 here, where he is compared to David, as well as Ps. 106.30-31 and 1 Macc. 2.26.

If ch. 50 is taken as an integral part of what precedes, then clearly the emphasis on priesthood becomes even greater. As we have noted already, Simon was a Zadokite, and by the time of the Greek translation of the book the Zadokites were no longer in power. It is presumably for this reason that at this point the Greek version differs significantly from the Hebrew. All the standard English translations follow the Greek, but at 50.24 the Hebrew has

> May he confirm with Simeon his love
> And raise up for him the covenant of Phinehas
> Which shall not be cut off for him or for his descendants
> Like the days of heaven.

(This is the translation offered by Hayward 1996: 43; see also p. 82 for a comparison with and appraisal of the Greek text.) In the Greek text vv. 22-24 look like a kind of appendix to the main poem, and NRSV does in fact, by double-spacing, separate these verses from what has preceded. Certainly in the Hebrew they form an integral part of the poem in praise of Simon. It is possible that, other, more subtle, changes can be detected between the two versions in their assessment of the priestly figures earlier in the Praise of the Ancestors: see Hayward 1996: 82 on possible modifications in ch. 45.

A number of interesting literary questions, much too wide-ranging to be explored here, are here raised concerning the extent to which a translation can properly be regarded as the 'same text' as its original.

Prophecy is perhaps less central within this material, but it is clear that the prophets are regarded as vital figures, particularly by the way in which they showed God's power at work. This seems to have been one of the reasons for giving prophetic status to those who are not described in those terms earlier in the tradition. Thus, Joshua is regarded as inheriting the prophetic office of Moses (46.1), though he is nowhere described as a prophet in the Hebrew Bible itself. Though the text is uncertain, it seems likely that Job is also given prophetic status here (49.9). (Thus NRSV, following the Hebrew; REB, which follows the Greek, has no reference to Job. The confusion is easily explained; the Hebrew name of Job, *iyyobh*, is formed from the same consonants as the Hebrew word for 'enemy' and the Greek understood the latter sense to be intended. Thus REB, 'the Lord remembered his enemies'.)

For those who were already esteemed in the tradition as prophets, particular emphasis is placed upon their miracle-working powers: Samuel (46.16-17); Elijah (48.1-6); and Elisha (48.12-14). The same is true of the presentation of Isaiah; as is noted by Barton 1986: 101, it is not so much for his words as for the miraculous powers that he showed (48.17-25) that Sirach wished to commend him to his audience. Jeremiah and Ezekiel are praised for their visionary capacity, but the lack of miracles associated with them may be the reason that they are dealt with much more summarily than Isaiah. In a similar way, 49.10, though it does provide us with what is probably our first reference to the 'Twelve Prophets' discerned as a collection of writings, is primarily interested in the way in which the bones of those prophets provide new life. It is, however, noteworthy that their function was perceived as being to comfort the people and offer them hope. This appears to be a reading of the 'Book of the Twelve' taken as a unity; to what extent this theme of comfort and hope is envisaged as extending to all the prophets is less easy to determine. (There are, of course, many other details in the presentation of individuals which deserve attention; in studying this part of Sirach the use of a commentary is more than usually desirable.)

Having looked at some specific aspects of this material the larger question now arises: Why is a historical survey of this kind found in Sirach at all? Sirach is a wisdom book, whose closest links in the Hebrew Bible are with Proverbs, and the lack of interest in Israel's history displayed by Proverbs is notorious. How should we explain this dramatic development?

Various proposals have been put forward. Martin 1986: 141 draws attention to an article of 1956 by Th. Maertens (not seen) which 'offered a Christian spiritual guide through Ben Sira's hymn', but— though the history of interpretation is an important study and the subject of much recent interest—that is probably rather distant from the concerns of most readers of this Guide. More immediately relevant may be the suggestion that the hymn could be understood as a claim on behalf of Scripture. Certainly at a somewhat later date Josephus and other writers regarded the possession of a distinct canon as one of the glories of Judaism; could Sirach be regarded as a precursor of this approach? Beckwith 1985: 73 is certainly inclined to this understanding, and he regards virtually the whole of our Hebrew Bible as traceable in the Hymn. His claim that it contains an allusion to the Psalms is

8. Praise of the Ancestors

perhaps optimistic, and he notes, without really resolving, the problem posed by the lack of reference to Daniel.

Another possibility is that proposed by Mack 1986. He sees in the Praise of the Ancestors a 'charter text' for the Judaism of his period. Thus understood, the hymn can best be seen as a weapon in the long struggle to show that Judaism could, as it were, defeat Hellenism on its own terms. It too had its epic heroes; it too could boast a history which showed a pattern in the working out of the divine will. A smaller-scale suggestion, published at about the same time as the work of Mack and therefore quite independent of it, is Lee 1986, who saw in these chapters an encomium on the high-priest Simon, with the hymn in whose honour the section concludes. Suggestions of this kind bring us back to the issue already discussed in Chapter 4 above. Does the use of literary forms consciously modelled on those of the Hellenistic world in itself imply a sympathetic attitude toward Hellenism on the part of Sirach himself?

However that may be, we can conclude this section by noting a further suggestion from Martin 1986. He draws attention, not only to the links with the apocalypses which we have already considered, but also to the fact of it being 'cult-centred historiography' (p. 155). He suggests, with a good deal of plausibility, that the interest in Sirach's Praise of the Ancestors is focused on those who were of special importance in the history of the cult: Aaron and Phinehas early on, then the great cultic reformers Hezekiah and Josiah among the kings of Judah, and from a later period Zerubbabel and Joshua. We may notice only that on this reconstruction the lack of reference to Ezra becomes still more striking; and that Martin's proposal to see 'the distinct possibility [of] a royal or priestly messianism' would not go unchallenged. That is a theme which we have already touched upon in Chapter 5 above, where some of the difficulties of definition were noted.

Further Reading

Barton, J.
1986   *Oracles of God: Perceptions of Ancient Prophecy in Israel after the Exile* (London: Darton, Longman & Todd).

Beckwith, R.
1985   *The Old Testament Canon of the New Testament Church* (London: SPCK).

Gammie, J.G.
1990   'The Sage in Sirach', in J.G. Gammie and L.G. Perdue (eds.), *The Sage in Israel and the Ancient Near East* (Winona Lake, IN: Eisenbrauns): 355-72.

Garbini, G.
    1988   *History and Ideology in Ancient Israel* (London: SCM Press).

Hayward, C.T.R.
    1990   'Rewritten Bible', in R.J. Coggins and J.L. Houlden (eds.), *A Dictionary of Biblical Interpretation* (London: SCM Press).
    1996   *The Jewish Temple: A Non-biblical Sourcebook* (London: Routledge).

Lee, T.
    1986   *Studies in the Form of Sirach 44–50* (SBLDS, 75; Atlanta: Scholars Press).

Mack, B.L.
    1986   *Wisdom and the Hebrew Epic: Ben Sira's Hymn in Praise of the Fathers* (Chicago: University of Chicago Press).

Martin, J.D.
    1986   'Ben Sira—a Child of his Time', in J.D. Martin and P.R. Davies (eds.), *A Word in Season: Essays in Honour of William McKane* (JSOTSup, 42; Sheffield: JSOT Press): 141-61.

Skehan, P.W., and A.A. Di Lella
    1987   *The Wisdom of Ben Sira* (AB, 39; New York: Doubleday).

Snaith, J.G.
    1967   'Biblical Quotations in the Hebrew of Ecclesiasticus', *JTS* NS 18: 1-12.

Soggin, J.A.
    1993   *An Introduction to the History of Israel and Judah* (London: SCM Press).

Torrey, C.C.
    1910   *Ezra Studies* (repr. 1970 with Prolegomenon by W.F. Stinespring; New York: Ktav).

9
ATTITUDE TO WOMEN

Human Women Negatively Judged

One of the most striking developments in biblical studies in recent years has been a new interest in the role played by and accorded to women in the different texts. Some feminist scholars have despaired of finding a positive evaluation of women anywhere, and have dismissed the biblical tradition as hopelessly androcentric. Others have been able to find a more positive attitude to women, sometimes in quite unexpected places. With Sirach, however, even the most optimistic researcher would find difficulty in evaluating his attitude to women positively. Wischmeyer 1995 is probably right in seeing in Sirach the intention of educating young men along the lines of the worldly conservative traditions of the Judaean upper classes. As we shall see in a moment, the teacher of such a group might feel that he had to alert them to the dangers posed by women.

Nevertheless women do play a prominent part in Sirach's thought. It has been calculated that more than 100 verses of the book deal with women, and it is not surprising in view of this new interest in the role of women that these verses have received detailed scrutiny. Already in a brief article in 1973 McKeating was able to suggest that many might regard Sirach as 'male chauvinist pig number one' (p. 85). He notes that Sirach's attitude was typical of his time, and typical also of what is known of other wisdom writings. The nagging wife, for example, comes high in the hate list of both Proverbs (e.g. 27.15) and Sirach (e.g. 25.20). (We might also mention that Josephus could run Sirach close in the chauvinist stakes, but that is not our present concern.)

McKeating does find some positive points, particularly the stress that

> a wife and a husband who live in harmony

are one of his three causes of pleasure (25.1). Whether Sirach's delight in feminine beauty (36.27) and 'shapely legs' (26.18) are to be counted in his favour would be more disputed. McKeating makes the interesting comment that in the modern Western world the usual perception is that women need protection from men. In Sirach's world, at least in the way that he presented it, women were regarded as the lustful sex against whose devices men had to be on the alert. It would not be difficult to see in this world-view a seed-bed for the characteristic world-rejecting anthropology of later Gnosticism.

It is in line with this that Camp 1991 has set out Sirach's view of women in honour/shame terms. Whereas for men their sexuality was perceived to be their honour, for women it was their shame. The values of such a world required that men must control women, in much the same way as, for example, they controlled financial dealings. Only thus would their honour be satisfied and recognized.

The most thorough investigation of this topic focusing specifically on Sirach is Trenchard 1982. He sets out the material relating to women under five heads: the woman as good wife; as mother and widow; as bad wife; as adulteress or prostitute; and as daughter. It is his judgment that even those statements that at first sight seem favourable in fact betray a negative evaluation of women and their role. Thus, in 26.1-4, 13-18 the 'good wife' is praised. But when this text is examined in greater detail, it quickly becomes apparent that a 'good' wife is seen as such entirely from her husband's point of view, in a manner reminiscent of the poem on the 'capable wife' which ends the book of Proverbs (Prov. 31.10-31). In both cases the wife is good because she is a desirable possession from her husband's viewpoint.

Similarly in 36.26-29 (36.21-26 in his enumeration of the verses) the wife is set out in terms of her desirability from the husband's viewpoint. This section is disputed in its detail, because the Hebrew and Greek texts here differ sharply from one another, but the general ethos of the section is not in question. In addition to these more extended passages there are several isolated sayings which can be grouped together as dealing with the good wife (7.19; 7.26a; 9.1; 25.8a; 28.15; 40.19, 23). Taken together they show that the good wife was regarded as a useful chattel. In 40.19, for example, her value is compared with cattle and orchards—useful possessions, all of them! Here, as in a number of other

9. Attitude to Women 87

examples, the full point of the comparison emerges only in the Hebrew text, and in older translations such as RSV, using only the Greek text, the comparison is somewhat less dismissive, for there the blameless wife is 'accounted better' than 'children and the building of a city'. Skehan and Di Lella 1987: 466 regard the textual change as no more than an error in transmission due to the similar beginnings of successive phrases ('homoioarchton' in the terminology of textual critics), but it is at least possible that there took place a deliberate modification of a comparison considered offensive. One has to admit, however, that there is not much evidence for a more positive attitude to women on the part of the Greek translator. In general the feeling is never far distant that to be a woman is in itself a negative situation.

This view is reinforced when we look at Trenchard's other categories. Even when a woman is pictured as a mother or a widow the portrayal is not particularly positive; mothers are usually only mentioned in parallelism with fathers, and it is clear that the father is the main subject of concern (e.g. 3.1-16). At one point (15.2) wisdom is likened to a mother, but this is a passing simile which is in no way developed. When we turn to widows, it seems as if a more positive picture might emerge, at least to the extent of a plea for sympathy for widows in their unenviable plight (e.g. 4.10), but even this is soon qualified: the widow is indeed not to be neglected, but the impression is given that this is to some extent necessary because of her nagging persistence ('she pours out her chatter' is Trenchard's translation of 35.17; one is reminded of the 'importunate widow' of Lk. 18.1-5).

Two of Trenchard's other three categories are viewed negatively through their very definition: bad wife, and adulteress or prostitute. The bad wife is the topic of the most extensive discussion, particularly in chs. 25–26. Trenchard rearranges 26.5-9 and 25.13-26 as a continuous poem. (Like many other scholars he regards 26.19-27, found only in the GII manuscript tradition and printed in italics in NRSV, as probably not part of the best text.) 26.5-9 give a strongly negative picture. Having already listed evils that are 'worse than death', the text then suggests that the presence of a 'bad wife' is something even worse still, with drunkenness and unchastity only to be expected. (It has led some male scholars to suppose that Sirach was himself married to a shrewish wife, though that seems an unnecessary conclusion.) In this context the traditional material used in 25.13-26 is given a strongly negative setting. Women are used as prime examples of all the evils envisaged. It is likely that 25.24 provides one of the earliest examples, indeed perhaps the first, of the association that has been so prominent ever since, particularly in the Christian tradition, which has laid great stress on the doctrine of 'the Fall', and essentially blaming it on Eve. 'From a woman sin had its beginning' makes no specific reference to Genesis 3, but it seems likely to have been in the author's mind here, with sin and death directly laid at her door. The only remedy for the unfortunate male is divorce (v. 26)! It is noteworthy that in this verse where NRSV has 'from yourself' the Greek would more literally be translated 'from your own flesh'. The language describing husband and wife as 'one flesh', going back to Gen. 2.24, is here given its own distinctive reading by Sirach.

In addition to this central block a number of isolated passages are in the same vein; in the praise of famous men (and as we saw in the last chapter it is taken for granted that it is men who deserve to be famous), it is the evil of women which is the cause of Solomon's downfall (47.19). If the Hebrew Bible is often androcentric, these texts go far beyond what is found there. Clearly Sirach's own warning against the use of abusive language (23.15) does not extend to his own language when used to describe women (e.g. 26.7-9).

Turning to a particular kind of 'bad wife', the punishment of the adulteress is set out in 23.22-27 in lurid detail. In one sense Sirach's view may be said to represent an 'advance' over what is found in the Hebrew Bible. There adultery appears to be condemned as an offence against another man's possession (his wife), an offence regarded as at least as severe as any sexual wrong-doing. Only in three late passages in the Hebrew Bible (Lev. 20.10; Ezek. 16.38; 23.45) is the verb *na'aph*, 'commit adultery', used in the feminine, and there it simply condemns the woman for conniving in the man's wrong practices. In Prov. 6.24 NRSV has 'adulteress', but REB 'loose woman' (though an unfortunate phrase) brings out the sense more accurately. At least in Sirach 23 the two sexes are treated equally, but whereas the woman is to be subject to public dishonour, the man's punishment is mainly an uneasy conscience. The shaming of the woman stands in marked contrast to the warnings to men against adultery in, for example, 9.8-9. The fault in the latter case largely lies with the woman whose 'shapeliness' leads the unthinking man astray. By contrast the unchaste woman is apparently to be judged by the way she makes up her eyelids! Numerous other passages (e.g. 9.3-4, 6-7; 19.2-3; 41.20) warn against the dangers posed by prostitutes.

But it is in fact the third category, the daughter, which attracts some of the most negative judgments. In 22.3-5 the possibility of a 'sensible

9. Attitude to Women

daughter' is allowed, though this will show itself only in the obtaining of a husband. But the passage's main concern is with the risks that a daughter poses to her father; even her birth is a loss. The likely result of a 'headstrong daughter' is sexual impropriety described in barely concealed obscenities (26.10-12). Perhaps the most remarkable passage is 42.9-14, setting out all the dangers posed by daughters and ending with the revealing assertion that

> Better is the wickedness of a man than a woman who does good;
> it is woman who brings shame and disgrace (42.14).

As Trenchard points out, there is little explicit discussion of daughters in the Hebrew Bible, and certainly nothing as negative as this. One wonders whether Sir Walter Scott had this passage in mind when in *Ivanhoe* he has the Templar who wishes to seduce the Jewish girl Rebecca describe her as 'gentle Ecclesiastica...daughter of Sirach'. If so, it would be an ironic reversal of the original author's point. In any case it is only when a daughter is safely married that a father can feel that his 'great task' is completed (7.25).

Taken overall, then, we may feel that Trenchard's picture is right when he notes how even the 'good wife' material is never really positive about the position of women, being always set out from the husband's viewpoint. The 'bad wife' received far more attention, and the daughter—astonishingly—receives the most negative treatment of all. Traditional material is often rearranged in negative ways, so as to justify Trenchard's conclusion (p. 173) that the book displays 'a personal negative bias against women'.

The most substantial treatment of the role of women in Hellenistic Judaism to have appeared since Trenchard's work is Archer 1990. Curiously, though her work was published eight years after that of Trenchard, she makes no reference to it. The structure of her work is different; she considers the references in the literature to the different stages of a woman's life, from early years to death, and there is thus no systematic treatment of Sirach. What she offers is therefore the provision of a chapter of social history rather than a specific study of Sirach. In this way she provides a valuable overview of the position of women in the Judaism of the last centuries BCE. Her conclusion is that a 'rigid patriarchy' was the typical social structure, so that Sirach reflects not so much Trenchard's suggested 'personal negative bias' as 'the attitude prevalent among the Jews of Graeco-Roman Palestine' (Archer 1990: 20).

Are we to say then that this patriarchy was simply an inevitable product of Sirach's world? Di Lella 1995 argues against such a view, by noting the contrast between Sirach and Judith, two works which may not be far apart in their date of composition. In Judith, whereas the men are pictured as feeble and cowardly, Judith is unquestionably the heroine, rescuing her people from oppression.

Woman Wisdom

It is interesting to note that where Trenchard, a male scholar, offers this thoroughly negative understanding of Sirach's view of women, two women scholars, writing more recently, have wished to qualify that judgment. In *The Women's Bible Commentary* we find the judgment that the references in Sirach 'provide some of the most positive as well as the most negative statements about women in the tradition' (Schuller 1992: 237). When explored in detail, this unexpected judgment relates mainly to the fact that, alongside the essentially negative verdicts on human women, wisdom is portrayed in feminine terms. We have already given some brief consideration to this picture of 'woman wisdom', and we shall certainly need to bear it in mind as we consider the theology of Sirach. More recently, McKinlay (1996: 176) has described Sirach's view of women as ambivalent; she gives greater weight than does Trenchard to the positive aspects of the presentation of the good wife. One is forced to admire the charitable viewpoint of these women writers, but it must be said that the overriding impression is undoubtedly a negative one.

More recently still Bergant has drawn interesting parallels between Sirach's suspicion of human women and his devotion to woman wisdom: 'There is no doubt about which woman Ben Sira would have one pursue; his teaching is quite clear. Choose Woman Wisdom!' (1997: 172). Here we are, of course, in the realm of reader–response criticism. It is highly improbable that Sirach would have thought of wisdom as a woman in any way comparable with feminine human beings. The comparison depends for its force on the insights brought by particular forms of modern study. As with reader–response criticism in general, some have welcomed it as offering new insights on traditional material; others have condemned it as dangerously subjective. Interesting hermeneutical questions arise as to the necessity, or even the propriety, of taking the original author's views into account when forming an appraisal of his work.

9. Attitude to Women

By way of postscript an interesting development in the history of interpretation may be noted. In the mediaeval Christian tradition, there developed an understanding of the Virgin Mary as the one possessed of true wisdom. It became customary to use Sirach 24, with its praise of (feminine) wisdom as one of the lessons in Masses devoted to the Virgin Mary. Mary was no longer regarded in that tradition as an 'ordinary woman', and readings likening her to divine wisdom were more appropriate than passages which pictured her as a human mother.

Further Reading

Archer, L.
1990 *Her Price Is beyond Rubies: The Jewish Woman in Graeco-Roman Palestine* (JSOTSup, 60; Sheffield: JSOT Press).

Bergant, D.
1997 *Israel's Wisdom Literature: A Liberation–Critical Reading* (Minneapolis: Fortress Press).

Camp, C.V.
1991 'Understanding a Patriarchy: Women in Second Century Jerusalem through the Eyes of Ben-Sira', in A.-J. Levine (ed.), *'Women like this': New Perspectives on Jewish Women* (Atlanta: Scholars Press): 1-39.

Di Lella, A.A.
1995 'Women in the Wisdom of Ben Sira and the Book of Judith: a Study in Contrasts and Reversals', in J.A. Emerton (ed.), *Congress Volume Paris 1992* (VTSup, 61; Leiden: E.J. Brill): 39-52.

McKeating, H.
1973–74 'Jesus ben Sira's Attitude to Women', *ExpTim* 85: 85-87.

McKinlay, J.E.
1996 *Gendering Wisdom the Host: Biblical Invitations to Eat and Drink* (JSOTSup, 216; Sheffield: Sheffield Academic Press).

Schuller, E.M.
1992 'The Apocrypha', in C.A. Newsom and S.H. Ringe (eds.), *The Women's Bible Commentary* (London: SPCK): 235-43.

Skehan, P.W., and A.A. Di Lella
1987 *The Wisdom of Ben Sira* (AB, 39; New York: Doubleday).

Trenchard, W.C.
1982 *Ben Sira's View of Women: A Literary Analysis* (BJS, 38; Chico, CA: Scholars Press).

Wischmeyer, O.
1995 *Die Kultur des Buches Jesus Sirach* (BZNW, 77; Berlin: W. de Gruyter).

10

THEOLOGICAL THEMES

We should begin our consideration of the theological significance of Sirach by noting that the important developments mentioned in Chapter 4 above with regard to renewed interest in the Judaism of the last centuries BCE have affected the use of the Apocrypha in the Christian tradition in recent years. Previously, it was largely neglected or at most regarded as 'background' to the New Testament. A number of recent studies have, however, given it a much more significant status. Thus the very title of an essay by Reimer is instructive: 'The Apocrypha and Biblical Theology'. The particular theme he pursues is that the New Testament understanding of divine forgiveness as being in some sense dependent upon human forgiveness is not characteristic of the Hebrew Bible, but is found in Sirach:

> Forgive your neighbour the wrong he has done,
> and then your sins will be pardoned when you pray (28.2).

Reimer (1996: 277-78) finds in this section of Sirach the 'basis for the parable [of the Unmerciful Servant] of Matt. 18.23-35'. He treats it as much more than background to the New Testament—it is itself an important element in the development of a biblical theology.

This example is intended only as illustrative. It shows that the apocryphal books, traditionally neglected in Protestant Christianity, are being treated with renewed interest. Sirach in particular may benefit from such interest. Within the context of the Hebrew Bible itself the Wisdom literature has often been regarded as something of an 'alien element' in theological terms, because of its failure to mention Exodus and Sinai, Davidic kingship and covenant. Both in ch. 24, where wisdom and Torah are identified, and in chs. 44–49, the praise of the

10. Theological Themes

ancestors, this supposed imbalance is put right. (It is, of course, another matter whether this is a fair perception of the earlier literature, but it is beyond dispute that it has been a widely held understanding.)

This renewal of interest means that a measure of selection is here necessary. We can only hope to outline some of the most characteristic theological themes. There are some important theological issues concerning which Sirach seems to have no distinctively new contribution to offer. Worship, for example, is taken for granted as an important component of the community's and the individual's life. The importance attributed to the priesthood, especially in the Praise of the Ancestors, has already been noted, and there are passages in the earlier part of the book where the importance of proper worship is stressed. But there is not much here that is new; all that one can say of a passage such as that starting at 34.21

> If one sacrifices ill-gotten goods, the offering is blemished,
> the gifts of the lawless are not acceptable

is that Sirach was familiar with the prophetic criticisms of false worship and stressed them for his own readers. Indeed, 35.1-4 seem to follow those prophetic criticisms even more strictly, with vv. 3-4 strongly reminiscent of Hos. 6.6:

> The one who returns a kindness offers choice flour,
> and one who gives alms sacrifices a thank-offering.

Clearly appropriate attitudes and behaviour towards one's neighbour are seen as at least an essential concomitant of true worship.

Again, though Sirach's attitude to the structures of society has serious limitations, as we saw in the last chapter, it is of a piece with much of what we find in the Hebrew Bible. It can certainly be regarded as an important theological theme and one which concerned our author greatly, but again here he is much more an upholder of what he hoped were established values than a developer of anything new.

There are, however, important developments which are much more distinctive in Sirach. He would almost certainly have been appalled to be told he was producing something 'new'; his aim will have been to bring out and clarify the implications of the tradition he had received. We may see some of what he said as new; he himself regarded it as an integral part of his inheritance. The theological points we shall be concerned with are found in all parts of the book, though they are much more prominent in the hymns and poems than in the proverb-like sayings. It is, however, in the latter that the emphasis on rewards and punishments, very characteristic of the book of Proverbs (and of course brought into question by Job and Qoheleth), finds its most characteristic expression, and we may touch on this briefly at this point.

A good deal of attention in Hebrew Bible scholarship has been devoted to what in German is commonly known as the 'Tun-Ergehen-Zusammenhang', which we may translate rather inelegantly as the 'act–consequence relationship'. Do human actions bring about the consequences that they deserve? Such a view is strongly upheld in Proverbs and in some Psalms (e.g. 37), but questioned in Job (where the very circumstances of the story preclude such an understanding) and regarded with scepticism in Ecclesiastes. But with Sirach we seem to revert to the older understanding:

> Whoever throws a stone straight up throws it on his own head...
> Whoever digs a pit will fall into it,
> and whoever sets a snare will be caught in it.
> If a person does evil it will roll back upon him (27.25-27).

As so often with assertions of this kind it is difficult to know whether the author has been extraordinarily fortunate in his experience, or is setting out religious maxims regardless of any contrary evidence.

In this point, as we have seen, Sirach follows an established tradition in the Hebrew Bible. But there are of course other theological emphases, where it appears as if he has something more distinctive to contribute. The most important of these concerns must be wisdom. Sirach has been described as 'the first to elaborate a true theology of wisdom in Israel' (Jacob 1978: 254). This manifests itself in creation, is linked with history, and has its most characteristic expression as the fear of the Lord.

The Fear of the Lord

It will be helpful now to consider each of these themes. We will take them in reverse order, beginning with the 'fear of the Lord'. Some scholars (e.g. Haspecker 1967) have argued that this rather than wisdom as such should be seen as basic. Certainly stress on the fear of the Lord is found in all parts of the book. It is a wide-ranging concept within the Hebrew Bible itself, being, for example, a characteristic of the messianic figure envisaged in Isa. 11.2-3. But its most usual context is the Wisdom literature, and it seems best to see Sirach's usage as a development of that found in Proverbs (1.7 and frequently) and Job 28.28. From the very outset (1.11-20) Sirach develops these characteristics, so that the god-fearing human being (in practice, of course, a man) is clearly his ideal, the embodiment of true wisdom. In the development of the poem it may well be that there are elements dependent on the picture of woman wisdom in Proverbs 1–9. (For detailed discussion see the commentary on these verses in Skehan and Di Lella 1987.) Nevertheless, there are limits in such a presentation, for, as we must remember, wisdom is presented not only as a feature of human behaviour at its best but also as a divine gift. It seems better, therefore, to regard any division between the fear of the Lord and wisdom as essentially a false dichotomy, and to understand the fear of the Lord primarily as the manifestation of wisdom (1.14). This will enable us to see in the setting out of his thoughts on wisdom the most striking development of the book.

History and Creation

The second of Jacob's topics is history, and here the obvious example is the praise of the ancestors, a series of examples of the power of wisdom. Jacob suggests that this was 'an original presentation of the history of Israel as it was taught in the schools of wisdom' (1978: 255). Evidence for this is lacking, as we have already seen. But in any case perhaps more remarkable is the way in which Sirach brings together themes which had previously not been integrated. The specific identification of wisdom as the covenant of God,

> the law that Moses commanded us
> as an inheritance for the congregations of Jacob (24.23)

makes it clear that the historical traditions of Israel are now interpreted in terms of wisdom.

When we come to consider Sirach's stress on the world as an ordered creation we find another extremely important aspect of his thought, one which is foundational to his understanding of wisdom. It is not always easy to decide when the reference is specific to Israel and when it is intended to be universal. The creation theme is found in chs. 16–17, both the totality of creation and the specific role of human beings. NRSV sets out the poem in ch. 17 as if knowledge/law/covenant (vv. 11-12) were given to the whole of humanity, but this may be better seen (Perdue 1994: 262) as a separate poem focusing specifically on the Jewish tradition.

The clearest expression of Sirach's understanding of the created order is found in the hymn-like passage beginning at 42.15: 'I will now call to mind the works of the Lord'. A vivid portrayal of the natural world follows. In one sense it ends at 43.33,

> For the Lord has made all things,
> and to the godly he has given wisdom.

In another sense, however, that 'ending' marks the preceding hymn off as in fact a prelude to the praise of the ancestors which follows. Their examples down the ages have been God's prime way of showing the potentialities of his creation.

Wisdom

All these points are important elements in helping us to picture the understanding of wisdom found in Sirach. If we now turn to consider the actual usage of the relevant terms, a very helpful analysis of the understanding of wisdom in Sirach is offered by Di Lella 1993. He notes that words with the *soph*-root occur 91 times in the GI manuscript tradition of the Septuagint, and in the surviving Hebrew the *hakam* root is found 104 times, evidence of the importance of the wisdom theme throughout Sirach.

Di Lella claims that it is possible to make a distinction between theoretical wisdom, which he sees as providing the underpinning of Sirach's thought, and practical wisdom, the outworking of which is more prominent in the book itself. One wonders whether a distinction along these lines is always helpful; theoretical and practical spheres merge into one another.

However that may be, there is an important balance to be maintained between the recognition of wisdom as a gift from God ('All wisdom is from the Lord', 1.1) and as something that is to be striven for by human efforts. To characterize wisdom as a gift from God might seem to imply that human beings can be idle, but such an attitude is strongly condemned (22.1-2). To achieve wisdom hard work is involved (6.18-37). The dichotomy between faith and works stressed in some Christian traditions finds no basis here!

Sirach's stress on education, which we have already noted several times, provides the natural context within which wisdom is to be acquired (ch. 39 is again relevant here). Properly cultivated, it will provide an assurance against false claims to wisdom (19.22-25). Whether the warnings in this last passage are specifically aimed against Hellenism remains uncertain, but in any case the Israelite context of true wisdom is emphasized.

All this material may properly be regarded as an anticipation of ch. 24, the hymn of self-praise, by wisdom. We have already noted the

10. Theological Themes

similarities with the Isis aretalogies, and certainly wisdom is pictured almost as if she were a goddess (!), in the context both of the people of God (v. 1) and of the heavenly council (v. 2). (Like chs. 1 and 16–17 this chapter is preserved only in Greek.) But the particular emphasis is on the way in which wisdom has been manifested to the people of God. Wisdom is represented as being told by the creator,

> Make your dwelling in Jacob,
> and in Israel receive your inheritance (24.8).

With this specific reference to Jacob/Israel the links with Proverbs 8, otherwise close in much of 24.1-22, begin to break down. Wisdom is already pictured as established in Zion, and her domain is Jerusalem (24.10-11), and in the great climax of the poem wisdom is identified with the Torah:

> the book of the covenant of the Most High God
> the law that Moses commanded us
> as an inheritance for the congregations of Jacob (24.23).

This last verse has been widely seen as the theological high-point of the work, though it is important to recognize the larger context within which it stands.

Wisdom comes from God, who is himself the truly wise one, and who formed wisdom as the first work of creation (1.1-10). She is also identified as the 'word' of God, an important theme in Hellenistic literature, though this identification is found only in the longer Greek text (1.5; cf. NRSV mg.). This text also identifies wisdom with the 'eternal commandments', that is, the Torah. Such a link had to some extent been adumbrated within the Hebrew Bible, particularly in Psalms 1 and 119, but it here becomes much more explicit.

Chs. 16–17 and 24 were focused upon by Sheppard 1980 as 'case studies' in exploring his contention that wisdom became *the* theological category through which the Torah and the Prophets came to be interpreted. Though Sheppard in no way plays down the links with Proverbs that we have considered earlier, he notes that there is no formal collection which could be regarded as 'the wisdom tradition'. 'Wisdom literature', as a description of part of the Hebrew Bible, usually Proverbs, Job and Qoheleth, is a modern scholarly usage. So 'the wisdom of all the ancients' (39.1) is not to be regarded as confined to what we should call 'wisdom books'. Indeed the suggestion has been made (Nickelsburg 1981: 56), that the stress on 'all the ancients' implies the wisdom lore of other parts of the ancient Near East as well as Israel itself. This seems unlikely in view of the stress on Israel's own traditions which pervades the whole book. When we consider wisdom in Sirach, therefore, we should reckon that it has its roots and antecedents not only in Proverbs, but in the whole range of biblical material. We have seen earlier (Chapter 6 above) how, in Sheppard's view, a variety of techniques was used by Sirach to set out a wisdom context for parts of the Hebrew Bible which would not normally be regarded as having reference to wisdom. As is implied by the title of his book, he regards wisdom as a 'hermeneutical construct', so that the Torah comes to be interpreted and understood as 'really' being about wisdom.

Whether or not one accepts the whole of Sheppard's reconstruction, it is clear that the understanding of wisdom and folly have developed beyond the perception of them found in the book of Proverbs. There, especially in chs. 10–22, they were often simply different ways of describing contrasting types of human behaviour. In Sirach, by contrast, wisdom and folly can be seen in the context of loyalty to the Torah or the failure of such loyalty. Hengel 1974: 141, describes this as the beginnings of a 'theological anthropology'. He goes on to suggest that part of the author's aim may have been to brand rival Jewish groups as mired in folly, but our knowledge of the society of the time is insufficient for this to be more than an interesting speculation.

The more specific identification of wisdom with the Torah in ch. 24 does not therefore come as a complete surprise. It is to some extent implicit in earlier parts of the book, and not only in those sections which Sheppard studied in detail; for example at 1.26 where wisdom is to be found in keeping the commandments, and at 19.20-24, where the links between wisdom and loyalty to the Torah are set out. In other words 24.23 should be seen as a climax of what has already been adumbrated earlier in the book. This is true both in the very specific Torah–wisdom link, and also in the exclusive claim on its possession being made for the Israelite community.

It is, of course, notorious that this passage stands at an important parting of the ways, which cannot be fully explored in the present context. Wisdom was given a new theological context, and it also opened the possibility of a more abstract, speculative type of development which was to lead (in the view of many) towards Gnosticism. In Judaism, perhaps the most striking development from the perception found here is in the works of Philo. In many ways even more striking is the carry-over to early Christianity, notably the wisdom-type Christology found in such New Testament writings as John and Colossians.

Sirach played an important part in the Christian tradition, particularly with regard to the Christological controversies that emerged in the fourth and fifth centuries. In later Christian tradition, Sirach comes to be quoted in the Latin tradition first by Cyprian, as we saw in the first chapter, and by various Greek fathers from Clement of Alexandria onwards. The subsequent history of interpretation shows some interesting developments, and is an area of study which has come to the fore in recent years, but it goes beyond our immediate concerns.

Other Theological Concerns

We may conclude by noting briefly that there are other important theological concerns in Sirach. It is well known that the issue of a future life became an important matter for reflection in the Judaism of the last centuries BCE, and it is instructive to consider Sirach's position on this topic. We noted above that Sirach's position within Judaism has been compared by some scholars to that of the later Sadducees, and one of the reasons for this is his rejection of any idea of a blessed future life. Such a passage as 17.27-28 expresses his view very clearly:

> Who will sing praises to the Most High in Hades?
> In place of the living who give thanks?
> From the dead, as from one who does not exist, thanksgiving has ceased:
> those who are alive and well sing the Lord's praises.

This passage could be paralleled elsewhere in the book (e.g. 14.11-19), but there are also some indications that this view was slightly modified at an early stage. The GII manuscript tradition has made some changes which imply that it is only the ungodly who may expect extinction at death. At 7.17, for example, the Hebrew text has 'for the expectation of mortals is worms', but this has been modified in the Greek to 'for the punishment of the ungodly is fire and worms' (cf. NRSV text and margin). Indeed, in the longer Greek text, belief in a future life is a frequent theme in the additional material. Thus NRSV and most modern translations omit 19.18-19. The latter of these verses reads in AV:

> The knowledge of the commandments of the Lord is the doctrine of life; and they that do things that please him shall receive the fruit of the tree of immortality.

This thought of immortality is not found in the Hebrew or the shorter Greek form of the book, and for the religious believer such a variety raises the question of the canonical form of the book which we discussed briefly in Chapter 1. The slightly later book, Wisdom of

Solomon, certainly looked forward to the prospect of immortality for the faithful servants of God, and it is possible that the tradition of Egyptian Judaism represented by the fuller Greek text of Sirach felt that some accommodation in that direction was desirable. (This is the work of the 'Pharisaic glossator' proposed by Box and Oesterley 1913: 285-87.)

This concern with life and death may lead us to one final theological concern of some importance. Sirach has a 'high' view of the possibilities open to humanity. This is most obviously embodied in his praise of the ancestors, men who had indeed been favoured by God but had also seized the opportunities that he offered to them. This conviction that human beings have a measure of free-will and are not simply the playthings of some unpredictable power, is an important element in Sirach's thinking. It is well expressed in 15.11-17. Typical is v. 15:

> If you choose, you can keep the commandments,
> and to act faithfully is a matter of your own choice.

We see here a different element of that potential for a 'theological anthropology' to which reference was made above. It seems an appropriate point at which to leave our consideration of this remarkable work.

Further Reading

Box, G.H., and W.O.E. Oesterley
    1913   'Sirach', in *APOT*, I, 268-517.
Haspecker, J.
    1967   *Gottesfurcht bei Jesus Sirach: Ihre religiöse Struktur und ihre doktrinäre Bedeutung* (AnBib, 30; Rome: Pontifical Biblical Institute).
Hengel, M.
    1974   *Judaism and Hellenism* (2 vols.; London: SCM Press).
Jacob, E.
    1978   'Wisdom and Religion in Sirach', in J.G. Gammie *et al.* (eds), *Israelite Wisdom: Theological and Literary Essays in Honor of Samuel Terrien* (Missoula, MT: Scholars Press): 247-60.
Di Lella, A.A.
    1993   'The Meaning of Wisdom in Ben Sira', in L.G. Perdue, B.B. Scott and W.J. Wiseman (eds.), *In Search of Wisdom: Essays in Memory of John G. Gammie* (Louisville, KY: Westminster/John Knox Press): 133-48.
Nickelsburg, G.W.E.
    1981   *Jewish Literature between the Bible and the Mishnah* (London: SCM Press).
Perdue, L.G.
    1994   *Wisdom and Creation: The Theology of Wisdom Literature* (Nashville: Abingdon Press).

Reimer, D.J.
1996 'The Apocrypha and Biblical Theology: The Case of Interpersonal Forgiveness', in J. Barton and D.J. Reimer (eds.), *After the Exile: Essays in Honour of Rex Mason* (Macon, GA: Mercer University Press): 259-82.

Sheppard, G.T.
1980 *Wisdom as a Hermeneutical Construct: A Study in the Sapientalizing of the Old Testament* (BZAW, 151; Berlin: W. de Gruyter).

Appendix A: The English Versions

This appendix sets out briefly the title given to our book, and the practice with regard to the enumeration of chapters and verses, of the main English versions. It should be noted that those versions which regard the Apocrypha as having no place in the biblical canon will have omitted our book from their translation; on these grounds it is also not normally included in editions of the Authorized (King James) Version published in the eighteenth and nineteenth centuries. It is probable that minor variations on what is set out below will be found in some editions of the different versions; no attempt has been made to research this point in detail.

Authorized (King James) Version Title: The Wisdom of Jesus the Son of Sirach or Ecclesiasticus (this last word in larger print and used in page headings). The full versification found in GII is found here, and may indeed be for many students the easiest way of tracing that fuller form.

Revised Version Title: As in AV. This version follows better Greek manuscripts, referred to as 'the best authorities' in the margin; these are the major Septuagint manuscripts from the fourth century CE or thereabouts, known to text-critics as B, S and A. There are therefore frequent omissions of verses, beginning with 1.5 and 7, and continuing throughout the book down to 50.29b. The omitted verses, some 150 in all, are not even included in the margins, and the revisers of the Apocrypha clearly felt greater freedom to make their own comments than was the case with the Old and New Testaments. Comments suggesting that the Greek text of particular passages is probably corrupt are not infrequent.

Revised Standard Version Title: Ecclesiasticus, or The Wisdom of Jesus the Son of Sirach, the last word being the one set out in larger fount and repeated for the page headings. The same verses are omitted as in RV, but in most cases their text is now included in the margin, usually in the form 'Other authorities add...'. This is the first version to have incorporated the evidence of the Hebrew text in any systematic form, though the base text is still the Greek. Hebrew is occasionally given preference (e.g. at 5.6, 'he will forgive', where Greek had 'he will be pacified'), and elsewhere the Hebrew has led to greater confidence in verses questioned by RV. Thus at 4.23 RV included the whole verse, but with a marginal note saying that most authorities omit the second half; RSV includes it, largely on the basis of the Hebrew reading.

Jerusalem Bible Title: Editions vary, but many simply have 'Ecclesiasticus' without further elaboration, though in the 'Introduction to the Wisdom Books' references are given in the form 'Si'. The translation is based on the Greek text, with Hebrew variants noted in the margin. The Greek text followed is the GI version, and the 'additional' verses of GII, beginning once again with 1.5, 7, are noted in the margin as 'additions'. In a number of cases, however, this is an inadequate way of making the points needed, and so we find in the side-margins of the Jerusalem Bible alternative verse numbers given: this can be extremely confusing. In ch. 1, for example, the marginal verse numbers go up to 40, yet no single manuscript contains so many. The high number is achieved by implied reference to every possible addition. Many such passages are not actually printed in ordinary editions, or regarded as 'additions', for in the judgment of the editors they form no part of the canonical text. (This is more important for the Jerusalem Bible, which is a Catholic version, giving canonical status to Sirach, than it is to translations in other traditions.) Of the various modern versions, the system of referencing used by the Jerusalem Bible seems to be the least accessible.

New Jerusalem Bible Title: Ecclesiasticus. It seems as if the difficulties mentioned above with regard to the Jerusalem Bible were taken into account when it was revised, and a preliminary note is now added explaining that the enumeration of the verses is based on a Latin text which contained several additions to the original. It is stated that in some cases whole verses are omitted in this edition.

New English Bible Title: Ecclesiasticus or the Wisdom of Jesus Son of Sirach. The first word is in larger type and is repeated for the individual page headings. This translation was consciously independent of the AV/RV/RSV tradition, and so some difference in usage might be expected. Nevertheless the pattern found with regard to verses is close to that of RSV, but with fewer marginal references to additions where these merely amplify existing verses.

Revised English Bible Though some changes have of course been made in the translation by comparison with NEB, it appears as if title and versification have not been altered.

New Revised Standard Version Title: Ecclesiasticus, or the Wisdom of Jesus Son of Sirach, with the last word in larger type and repeated throughout the page headings. A number of sub-headings which are found in some forms of the Greek text are here for the first time included in an English version. The versification has been modified in a few cases (e.g. ch. 2 has 17 as against 18 verses), but the marginal comments are similar to those in RSV. But the NRSV not only gives more weight to the Hebrew in its choice of the best rendering; it also includes the psalm-like passage found in Hebrew but no Greek manuscripts between 51.12 and 13.

From the above it will become clear that no consensus has yet been reached, either as to the appropriate title to be used, or in details of versification. The standard warning that all references should be carefully checked is nowhere more necessary than here. For those who wish to compare four of the most widely used recent translations a valuable resource is *The Complete Parallel Bible* (Oxford: Oxford University Press, 1993), which sets out in parallel columns the texts of the New Revised Standard Version, the Revised English Bible, the New American Bible, and the New Jerusalem Bible. This enables one to see at a glance that the psalm-like passage in the Hebrew text following 51.12 is included in NRSV and NAB only.

Appendix B: Survey of Research

Many of the books and articles noted at the end of each chapter contain further bibliographical information. Particular mention should, however, be made of two recent survey articles which will be of special value to those who want to take further their studies of particular aspects of Sirach. These are:

D.J. Harrington, 'Sirach Research since 1965: Progress and Questions', in J.C. Reeves and J. Kampen (eds.), *Pursuing the Text: Studies in Honour of Ben Zion Wacholder on the Occasion of his Seventieth Birthday* (JSOTSup, 184; Sheffield: Sheffield Academic Press, 1994), pp. 164-76.

A.A. Di Lella, 'The Wisdom of Ben Sira: Resources and Recent Research', in *Currents in Research: Biblical Studies* 4 (1996), pp. 161-81.

Harrington devotes more than half of his article to textual problems, raising some interesting methodological questions, whether the Hebrew and Greek texts should be treated as separate entities or used to construct an eclectic text. He then considers 'Setting in Life and Sources' with special attention to the work of Middendorp noted in Chapter 4 above; and concludes with discussion of various themes of the book: 'fear of the Lord', inclination and free will, and so on.

Di Lella, by contrast, ranges more widely, being more directly concerned to present information. So his article is for the most part a very extensive listing of recent books, articles, Festschrift essays and the like. Most of these are listed without comment, but in a number of cases Di Lella highlights the particular concerns of the item addressed. He concludes by commenting in greater detail on instruments of study: editions of the texts in their various languages; concordances and the like, including various computer programs; and sets out certain desiderata in textual matters and modes of reference. Details of the computer programs which Di Lella himself has used are provided in footnotes 2 and 3 of his article 'The Meaning of Wisdom in Ben Sira', in L.G. Perdue,

B.B. Scott and W.J. Wiseman (eds.), *In Search of Wisdom: Essays in Memory of John G. Gammie* (Louisville, KY: Westminster/John Knox Press, 1993), pp. 133-48. They are not reproduced here; material that was up to date in work published in 1993 will no doubt have been rendered obsolete by the onward march of computer technology. The articles by Harrington and Di Lella will be essential stand-bys for those who wish to pursue detailed research on Sirach. As far as it has proved possible to judge they have the inestimable benefit for tools of this kind in being accurate in their detailed references.

Other Reference Tools

With regard to reference works, it is also appropriate to mention that the *Dictionary of Classical Hebrew*, edited by D.J.A. Clines, currently appearing from the Sheffield Academic Press (at the time of writing three volumes have been published), includes the Hebrew text of Sirach as part of its database. Earlier dictionaries often refer to Sirach, but for the most part only on an illustrative basis. For those concerned with the relation of the different linguistic traditions, a useful tool is available in D. Barthélemy and O. Rickenbacher, *Konkordanz zum Hebräischen Sirach* (Göttingen: Vandenhoeck & Ruprecht, 1973). For the Greek version the long-standard work of Hatch and Redpath, first published in 1897, has recently become available once more in a two-volume edition: E. Hatch and H.A. Redpath, *A Concordance to the Septuagint* (2 vols.; Grand Rapids: Baker Book House, 1987). For those dependent on English versions, no concordance embracing NRSV has been published at the time of writing, but there is available *A Concordance to the Apocrypha/Deuterocanonical Books of the Revised Standard Version* derived from the databank of the Belgian Abbey of Maredsous and published by Eerdmans and Collins in 1983.

INDEXES

INDEX OF REFERENCES

Old Testament
Genesis
1–3	65
2.10-13	68
2.11-14	56
2.24	88
3	88

Exodus
30	67

Leviticus
20.10	88

Numbers
25	81

Deuteronomy
33.4	67

2 Samuel
24.14	64

2 Chronicles
13.22	70
16.12	45

Ezra
4.8–6.18	33
7–10	80

Nehemiah
8	80
9.6–37	78
13.23-24	42

Job
15.17	63
28	70, 75, 76
28.28	94

Psalms
1	97
37	94
78	78
105	78
106	78
106.16-18	79
106.30-31	81
119	97
135–136	78
136	26

Proverbs
1–9	28, 75, 95
1.7	65, 94
6.24	88
8	15, 70, 76, 97
8.22-31	75
8.30	75
10–31	14, 27
10–22	98
22.17–24.22	47
24.19-20	66
26.27	66
27.15	85
31.10-31	26, 86

Ecclesiastes
3	63
12.12	63
12.13	63

Isaiah
11.2-3	94

Jeremiah
10.11	33

Ezekiel
16.38	88
23.45	88

Daniel
2–6	80
2.4–7.28	33

Hosea
6.6	93

2 Esdras
14.45	20

Wisdom of Solomon
10.1–11.4	79

Sirach
1–43	27
1–24	19
1–23	26
1	28, 97, 99
1.1–10.3	31
1.1–10	97
1.1	96
1.5-7	17

Sirach

1.5	102, 103	14.18	51	25.8	86	
1.7	65, 102, 103	14.20–23.27	29	25.13–34.8	31	
1.1–4.19	29	14.20-27	24	25.13-26	87	
1.11-30	29	15.2	87	25.20	85	
1.11-20	94	15.9–18.14	65	25.24	87	
1.14	95	15.11–18.14	29	25.26	88	
1.20	75	15.11-17	100	26.5-9	87	
1.25	23	16–17	67, 95, 97	26.7-9	88	
1.26	98	16.26	29	26.1-4	86	
1.28-30	29	17.1	29	26.10-12	89	
2	104	17.27-28	99	26.13-18	86	
2.1	28	17.32	59	26.18	86	
2.12-14	24	18.1	29	26.19-27	87	
2.17-18	17	18.30–23.27	31	27.25-27	94	
2.17	64	18.30	30	27.25-26	66	
3.1-16	27, 87	19.2-3	88	28.2	92	
3.1	16, 28	19.18-19	99	28.15	86	
3.12	28	19.20-24	98	29.24	60	
3.17	28	19.20	63	30.25-33.13	18	
4	19	19.22-25	96	31.1-4	18	
4.1	28	20.27	30	31.12–32.13	48	
4.10	87	21.15-28	75	31.12-14	48	
4.11–6.17	29	22.1-2	96	31.16	59	
4.23	103	22.3-5	88	33.7-13	72	
5.6	103	23	88	33.13–36.13	18	
6.18–14.19	29	23.7	30	33.16	56, 62	
6.18-37	96	23.15	88	33.19–42.14	19	
7	49	23.22-27	88	33.19–38.23	30	
7.4-7	49	24–43	26	34.9-13	71	
7.17	99	24	15, 25, 36, 67, 68, 76, 91, 92, 96-98	34.11-12	51	
7.18-36	28			34.13–36.17	31	
7.19	86			34.21	93	
7.25	89			35.1-9	49	
7.26	86	24.1–33.18	30	35.1-4	93	
7.27-28	28, 29	24.1–25.12	31	35.17	87	
8.1-2	29	24.1-22	97	35.21-26	24	
9	28	24.1-2	97	35.22-26	68	
9.1	86	24.1	25	36.1-22	18, 19	
9.3-4	88	24.6	76	36.1-21	24	
9.6-7	88	24.8	97	36.1-17	58	
9.8-9	88	24.15	67	36.18–42.14	31	
9.11	66	24.19	76	36.26-29	86	
10.1-5	49	24.23	60, 63, 67, 95, 97, 98	36.27	86	
10.4–18.29	31			38–39	48	
12	29	24.25-27	56	38.1-15	45	
14.3-19	49	25–26	30, 87	38.16-23	24	
14.11-19	99	25.1–33.18	19	38.24–43.33	31	
14.17-19	24	25.1	86	38.24–39.11	46, 47	

Index of References

38.24	48	45	81	51.13-30	25, 26, 71
38.32	48	45.6-25	49	51.13-20,30	34
38.34–39.11	71	45.6-22	80	51.23-25	72
39	72, 96	45.23-25	81	51.23	17, 70, 71
39.1-11	74	45.24-25	80		
39.1-2	63	46.1	81	*Baruch*	
39.1	97	46.16-17	82	4	77
39.4	46	47.17	66		
39.16	63	47.19	88	*1 Maccabees*	
39.27–43.30	35	48.1-6	82	2.26	81
40.19	86	48.12-14	82	2.51-60	79
40.23	86	48.17-25	82		
40.28	52	49	79	New Testament	
41.5-10	50	49.9	81	*Matthew*	
41.20	88	49.10	82	18.23-35	92
42.9-14	89	49.13	80		
42.15–49.16	19	49.14	74	*Luke*	
42.15–43.33	24, 31	49.16	26, 78	1.1-4	13
42.15	63, 95	50	19, 49, 78, 81	10.7	60
43.27	52			18.1-5	87
43.33	95	50.1-24	26		
44–49	42, 56, 92	50.1-4	45	*Acts*	
44–50.24	26	50.20-24	81	7	78
44–49	78	50.25-29	26	18.3	48
44.1	25	50.27	16, 46, 49, 68		
44.2	78			*2 Thessalonians*	
44.3-6	79	50.29	102	3.10	48
44.16	74	51	18, 26, 37		
44.17	35	51.1-12	24	*Hebrews*	
44.18	80	51.1	25	11	78
44.20	80	51.12-13	104		
44.22	80	51.12	35, 58		

INDEX OF AUTHORS

Archer, L. 90-91
Argall, R.A. 74

Baillet, M. 34
Barr, J. 45
Bartlett, J.R. 20, 43
Barton, J. 69, 83
Baumgartner, W. 23-24
Becker, J. 60
Beckwith, R. 21, 83
Ben-Hayyim, Z. 37
Bergant, D. 24, 91
Blenkinsopp, J. 26, 49
Boccaccini, G. 35, 74
Boman, T. 45
Box, G.H. 9, 15, 18, 34, 35, 58, 59, 100
Brockington, L.H. 15

Camp, C.V. 86
Caquot, A. 57
Charles, R.H. 43
Coggins, R.J. 50
Cook, S.L. 73
Crenshaw, J.L. 64

Danby, H. 21, 22
Davies, P.R. 74
Delcor, M. 24
Dell, K.J. 63
Di Lella, A.A. 9, 27, 28, 29, 30, 31, 32, 34, 35, 36, 37, 40, 46, 49, 51, 79, 90, 91, 95, 96, 100, 105-106

Eissfeldt, O. 15, 20
Epstein, L. 21

Flint, P.W. 34

Gammie, J.G. 24-25, 37, 66, 79
Garbini, G. 80
Gilbert, M. 19, 21, 60
Grabbe, L.L. 10, 14, 44

Harrington, D.J. 105-106
Haspecker, J. 94
Hayward, C.T.R. 44, 45, 80, 81
Heaton, E.W. 62, 71, 73-74
Hengel, M. 9, 10, 18, 44, 49, 50, 51, 52, 54, 98
Humbert, P. 47

Jacob, E. 47, 94, 95, 100

Kieweler, H.V. 50
Knox, W.L. 30

Lang, B. 36, 48, 51
Lee, T. 78, 83, 84
Lévi, I. 37
Levison, J.R. 29, 65

Mack, B.L. 13, 83, 84
McKeating, H. 85-86
McKinley, J.E. 30, 76, 77, 90, 91
Maertens, Th. 82
Marböck, J. 46
Martin, J.D. 58, 74, 79, 82, 83
Middendorp, Th. 50, 51, 52, 59, 65
Milik, J.T. 34
Murphy, R.E. 9, 24

Nelson, M.A. 38
Neusner, J. 57
Nicklelsburg, G.W.E. 30, 50, 97

Index of Authors

Oesterley, W.O.E. 15, 18, 34, 35, 58, 100

Pautrel, R. 52
Perdue, L.G. 95

Rad, G. von 9, 73
Rahlfs, A. 49
Reimer, D.J. 92
Ringgren, H. 75
Rüger, H.P. 34

Sanders, J.A. 34
Sanders, J.T. 47, 52, 53
Schechter, S. 63
Schuller, E.M. 90
Schürer, E. 24, 38
Scott, R.B.Y. 70
Sheppard, G.T. 64, 66, 67, 97, 98
Skehan, P.W. 9, 16, 17, 26, 27, 30, 34, 35, 36, 46, 49, 51, 79, 87, 95
Smend, R. 9, 50

Snaith, J.G. 9, 31, 62, 63, 64, 65, 80
Soggin, J.A. 80
Spicq, C. 9
Sundberg, A.C., Jr 60

Taylor, C. 63
Tcherikover, V. 50
Torrey, C.C. 80
Trenchard, W.C. 86, 87, 89, 90

Vattioni, F. 37
Vaux, R. de 34

Whybray, R.N. 71
Williams, D.S. 19
Williams, R.J. 50
Wischmeyer, O. 85

Yadin, Y. 35

Ziegler, J. 17, 18, 37, 49

www.ingramcontent.com/pod-product-compliance
Lightning Source LLC
Chambersburg PA
CBHW061420300426
44114CB00015B/1999